AMERICAN FREEDOM
AND THE RADICAL RIGHT

American Freedom and the Radical Right

Edward L. Ericson

90-038

FREDERICK UNGAR PUBLISHING CO.

New York

Library of Congress Cataloging in Publication Data

Ericson, Edward L.
    American freedom and the radical right.

    Includes index.
    1. Civil rights—United States.   2. Conservatism—
United States.   I. Title.
JC599.U5E68   323.4′0973   81-71132
ISBN 0-8044-5355-1   AACR2
ISBN 0-8044-6141-4 (pbk.)

CONTENTS

Preface

Freedom can prosper for a thousand years and die in a single generation. Those who live securely in the shelter of a centuries-old heritage may awaken to find themselves outcasts and aliens in their own house. It has happened to many outstanding elected officials, including well-known conservatives. A similar fate may threaten all those who believe in an open, pluralistic society.

From the radical right have come bitter attacks on "the religion of secular humanism." What do they mean by that often misunderstood phrase, and what is "secular humanism" anyway? Is it a good thing, or should we fear and condemn it?

That is what this book is about. It is an attempt to clarify the true issues of our day and to remind Americans of the immense importance of their heritage. It is my hope that this volume will stimulate deeper interest in exploring our constitutional character as a nation, which in turn will provide the basis for a defense against the current attack on secular, pluralistic democracy. Americans need to understand the roots of our moral and political freedom in the historic philosophy of liberalism as it was developed from Locke to Jefferson, especially by the English and Scottish moral philosophers. This subject is treated in some detail in Chapter 9.

The book developed from a number of my lectures on the threat of the radical right delivered during 1980 and 1981 at the New York Society for Ethical Culture. The bulk of the text, however, has been written anew, although some portions were also adapted for oral presentation and have been printed elsewhere. Much of the quoted material not identified as to source originated in forums or presentations at the Ethical Society and appeared in the *Moral Democracy Bulletin,* edited by Betty Brout. The *Bulletin* is the organ of the Center for Moral Democracy, which I organized and initiated at the Society and serve as director. I acknowledge with special appreciation an interview of Leo Pfeffer by Ms. Brout and an article for the *Bulletin* contributed by Lisa Desposito of Catholics for a Free Choice. My thanks go to Dr. Howard Kirschenbaum of the National Coalition for Democracy in Education for making available to me his statement in defense of humanistic education. I am also grateful to former Senator Frank Church and Dr. Carl Flemister, Executive Minister of the American Baptist Churches of Metropolitan New York for speaking at a public rally at the Society in defense of religious tolerance and pluralistic democracy. Their statements have been quoted extensively.

Finally, I owe an expression of appreciation to my office staff for their invaluable help: Dee Slosser and Doris Cattell, who typed the manuscript, and Donna Fetonte and Shirley Greiff, who assist the Center in many ways. May I also thank a Center volunteer and research librarian, Edith Levitt, who provided much useful material, and the many others who contributed their services.

The publisher, Frederick Ungar, who invited me to write this book, by his generous encouragement made possible the completion of the work against a stringent publication deadline. My thanks to him and to his staff for many valuable suggestions.

EDWARD L. ERICSON

New York, N.Y.
January, 1982

1

RESURGENT McCARTHYISM:
Today's Threat to Freedom

Those old enough to remember the early 1950s know the terrible price the American nation paid for the witch hunt known as McCarthyism. Senator Joseph McCarthy's seemingly casual but extravagant accusation of conspiracy and subversion wrecked lives, divided communities, intimidated and manipulated governmental agencies, and distorted and jeopardized the nation's foreign and domestic policy.

Many years were needed to overcome the damage done to our institutions and to restore the legal protection of the Bill of Rights. Senator McCarthy did not inflict this damage alone. He did not even initiate the hysteria remembered in his name. He was, in fact, a comparative latecomer to the scene, a skillful and ruthless opportunist who seized the moment to feed the inclination of many Americans to see their neighbors as conspirators, foreign agents, and traitors to their country.

The fears and discontents of the time required a devil to explain what appeared to be wrong with America, and McCarthy and thousands of his imitators gave them the devil they were looking for. That devil was "subversion," likely to be personified in the schoolteacher imprudent enough to encourage students to think and to question, the union organizer bold enough to go into a southern textile mill to organize, the clergyman outspoken enough to address issues of social justice or racial discrimination, or an editor courageous enough to expose venality and corruption.

The new version of McCarthyism now descending on the land is making its appearance under religious auspices, a sponsorship that compounds its viciousness. Like the earlier McCarthyites, these new witch hunters require a devil. And whether we like it or not, Americans who do not share their theological enthusiasm and moral absolutes have been elected to play the role of Satan—the evil, corrupting force of American life. Specifically that force is identified as "the religion of secular humanism." What is meant is any belief the new fundamentalists regard as unbiblical or "liberal"— especially beliefs and habits of thinking derived from modern science or the Age of Enlightenment.

The term "secular humanism" comes from a 1961 landmark opinion (*Torcaso vs. Watkins*) of the United States Supreme Court, which declared that those who hold ethical or nontheistic humanist beliefs are entitled to the same constitutional rights of religious freedom as those holding traditional beliefs. This straightforward application of the First Amendment to protect religious freedom for all deeply rankles those who think the religious protection clause of the Constitution should be restricted to traditional theological belief, in practice the freedom to be religious the "fundamentalist" Christian way, but not the freedom to be protected in holding differing beliefs.

In their confusion of issues the propagandists of the religious New Right charge that the public schools are promoting secular humanism as a state religion. According to their logic, if the state refrains from promoting prayer in the school, or does not teach the biblical account of creation, this restraint is tantamount to establishing humanism as the state religion. Since the Supreme Court noted that humanistic religions exist in the United States and are equally entitled to recognition as religions, the religious right makes a gigantic leap to the conclusion that all humanistic beliefs and values are religious. (It would be equally sensible to argue that since some dietary laws are religiously derived, all considerations of diet must be regarded as religious.)

The murkiness of this line of reasoning serves the objective of the demagogue who would use religion to dominate the political process and the public school. In short, we are faced with the prospect that a well-organized (and richly financed) right-wing crusade, disguised as a Christian revival, will increasingly dominate the political process and undercut the pluralistic character of American religious and social life.

Humanists and "liberals" are held responsible for the wreckage of the American family and the "decadence" of the nation. One remembers that in the last days of the Weimar Republic, before the rise of Hitler to power, liberals and "cosmopolitans" were similarly assailed by extremists of both left and right as the authors of social decay and corruption.

Thus, while most Americans have gone complacently about their business, the forces of intolerance have been gathering their forces in a movement toward religious distrust and intolerance. This organized threat to religious liberty goes by many names: the Moral Majority, the Christian New Right, the New Fundamentalism. Whatever the name, it preaches distrust of religious pluralism and secular democracy.

The foremost champion of this cult of intolerance has described Americans who hold a liberal or humanistic philosophy in terms that invite scorn and rejection. The Reverend Jerry Falwell declares: "The godless minority of treacherous individuals . . . must now realize they do not represent the majority. They must be made to see that moral Americans . . . will no longer permit them to destroy our country with their godless, liberal philosophies."

Another leader of the authoritarian right, Gary Potter, leader of Catholics for Christian Political Action, states baldly that liberalism is a sin, a rebellion against God, to which Falwell adds, "Secular humanism is nothing but communism waiting in the wings to be crowned with its political rights."

Jean Belsante, a spokeswoman of a group calling itself Citizens United for Responsible Education is even more direct in pointing an accusing finger at specific liberal religious, educational, and civic groups. Such people are part of an organized network, she alleges, which has been "working for decades to eradicate every trace of the Judeo-Christian heritage from our national life." She goes on gravely:

> This network is directed by an anti-God leadership that manipulates such organizations as the American Humanist Association, the American Ethical Union, the Unitarian Universalist Association, and the American Civil Liberties Union—the latter acting as the cartel's legal arm. The cartel works in concert with scores of atheistic "front-groups" including a number of "social health" agencies such as Planned Parenthood.

Such allegations, which informed people recognize as prejudice and calumny, could be ignored if they were not highly effective in poisoning the minds of the uninformed. Even fatuous accusations are repeated and believed. Appeals to distrust and intolerance stir interreligious misunderstanding, making the country ripe for political extremism and social polarization.

But why is humanism so often singled out as the great devil of the new fundamentalists? Sixty years ago the grandfathers of today's religious right deplored modernism and Darwinism. They still deny the overwhelming evidence for human evolution, as we shall see in a later chapter. Humanism is simply the current expression of their old bête noire, the spirit of free inquiry and scientific thinking applied to the problems of personal and social living, something they fear and seek to suppress.

Probably not one fundamentalist in a thousand could have defined a humanist before the Jerry Falwells, James Robisons, and others like them made humanism a code word for infidelity, moral indifference, and selfishness. While it is flattering to a handful of humanistic philosophers and religious liberals to have such inordinate influence attributed to them, this inflated attack cannot simply be shrugged off as a bad joke played upon the ignorant. For the moment "secular humanists" make an adequate devil, despite their limited numbers and power.

But as the authoritarian rightists flex their muscles and acquire a measure of political power they will require other devils. Moderate political and business leaders, and even responsible conservatives, will not be immune from their venom. We should recall that President Dwight D. Eisenhower and his Secretary of the Army Robert T. Stevens were the ultimate targets of McCarthy; true believers on the far right still nurture the myth that Eisenhower and his principal aides were part of a worldwide Communist conspiracy that they project into every department of government and society from the White House to the playground.

Former President Jimmy Carter, a twice-born evangelical Christian of undoubted sincerity (probably the most religious president in our history), was detested with special fervor for his loyalty to the Constitutional principle of church-state separation and opposition to an antiabortion amendment.

The witch hunt from the right is being conducted in the name of preserving the family, of protecting youth from corrupting influences, of fighting communism and godlessness, and of securing the Christian character of American institutions.

In what sense, we must ask, is the United States a Christian nation? Christianity is certainly the faith of the majority of American citizens, but no religion can claim legal standing as the "American" religion. As early as the administration of George Washington, our first President assured an Islamic nation of North Africa that the American government is not a Christian state, that the United States is neutral in matters of creed.

Supported by a consistent history of judicial decision, legal scholars agree that constitutionally and philosophically the American system is a secular democracy. That foundation is the surest safeguard of freedom. The most deeply religious citizen, equally with the nonreligious, has a stake in preserving the neutral character of the American government with respect to religious belief. Only a secular government can consistently and evenhandedly protect the religious freedom and equality of all its citizens.

Religious and philosophical liberals, including many devoted members of mainline churches, arouse the displeasure of the zealots of the New Right because the liberal tradition rejects spiritual authoritarianism, curtailment of the exercise of the free mind, intolerance, resort to the censorship of ideas, and the effort to distort or control the teaching of science. But it is not only humanists and religious liberals who have reason to be alarmed by the resurgence of organized intolerance.

Conservative believers have at least as much at stake. A distinguished United States Senator, Mark Hatfield of Oregon, long recognized for his fervent Christian faith, was reproved during the 1980 political campaign for declaring that while he is a conservative in religion, he is a liberal in social philosophy. The senator was castigated for supposing that as a Christian he could support principles of public policy that allow other citizens to follow other beliefs, especially on such sensitive issues as abortion.

Senator Hatfield is not the only public official to discover that the militants of the New Right are prepared to punish and destroy their coreligionists in public life who do not toe their line of religious intolerance. Yet evangelical Christians and other religious conservatives, such as Jimmy Carter and Mark Hatfield, who stand up to the zealots of the New Right, are simply upholding the historic principle of their own spiritual heritage.

We should remember that the concept of liberty of conscience is not the invention of modern religious liberalism or humanism. Consider, for example, the history of the largest body of evangelicals in the United States, the Baptists. Among the earliest independent evangelicals in Britain and the continent of Europe, Baptists were frequently flogged, jailed, and sometimes burned at the stake for their beliefs.

Three hundred years ago the rallying cry among these persecuted dissenters was "soul freedom"—the beginning of the struggle to separate church and state. The journal of George Fox, founder of the Quakers, indicates that Fox was inspired by his early contacts with the Baptists to embrace the idea of religion by personal conviction, thus providing the foundation for the Quaker experiment of liberty of conscience in Pennsylvania.

The two foremost figures in the early Baptist struggle for religious freedom were Roger Williams, who established the colony of Rhode Island as a haven for the persecuted, and his English contemporary John Bunyan, author of *Pilgrim's Progress*, the captivating allegory of spiritual suffering and deliverance that many critics place next to the English Bible and Milton's *Paradise Lost* among the devotional masterpieces of our tongue.

Much of *Pilgrim's Progress* was written in prison, where Bunyan was confined for his unlawful preaching as a nonconformist minister. When he vividly paints the awful martyrdom of Faithful, burned to dust before the eyes of his companions, Bunyan is recalling the recent experience of evangelical dissenters not far removed from his generation. Only sixteen years before Bunyan's birth, the last heretic in England to die at the stake, a Baptist, was burned in Litchfield. Bunyan well knew that he and his fellow nonconformists could easily be consumed in a revived firestorm of persecution. Their answer to this threat was a powerful appeal for religious liberty and the separation of church and state.

Thomas Jefferson had in view this history of suffering and the continuing persecution of Baptists and other dissenters in Virginia when he labored to disestablish the Anglican church, producing the enactment of the Virginia Act for Religious Freedom, the model for the First Amendment to the United States Constitution.

Sadly, as so often in history, the persecuted become the persecutors. New Right zealots have become especially conspicuous among fundamentalist Baptists and similar evangelical groups of the South and Midwest. Even so, the majority of evangelical Christians and their official church bodies continue to reject the role of persecutor and maintain their historic allegiance to religious liberty and church-state separation.

New Right preachers would like to capture this multitude of evangelicals, turning the traditional beliefs and cultural values of this widely distributed religious culture toward extremist political ends. If religious liberals, moderates, and secularists do not make the effort to understand this growing population and respond sympathetically to their largely southern and rural history and culture, the upwardly mobile evangelicals may strike out in rage at what they often interpret as contempt for their values. The far right attempts to present liberals and humanists as people who despise the faith and life style of evangelicals, as cynics and voluptuaries who would destroy the moral fiber of America and would reimpose the religious repression that evangelicals remember from the distant past. These fears and misrepresentations must be answered.

There is one principle upon which the sincere nonbeliever and believer can readily stand in accord: All can agree there is no teaching in the Bible, Jewish or Christian, of a "moral majority." Conformity and forced religiosity are the enemies of true spiritual commitment. The Jewish and Christian scriptures emphatically repudiate the smugness and hypocrisy of religious elites.

The prophets of Israel gave their lives denouncing popular idolatry—the practices and feast days of the "moral majority" of their time. The man from Nazareth condemned outward displays of piety altogether, forbidding public prayer. Bertrand Russell, skeptic and humanist that he was, cherished the text that his grandmother wrote on the flyleaf of the Bible she presented to him in his childhood: "Thou shalt not follow a multitude to do evil."

It is not a bullying "majority"—following a multitude to do evil—that points the way to spiritual renewal in America. True religion consists of works of justice and love—of meeting the needs of the poor, providing care for the sick, upholding the rights of the disadvantaged and the despised. "Blessed are the peacemakers for they shall be called the children of God," says a verse from the Sermon on the Mount, a teaching now being mocked by the political preachers of religious intolerance.

Citizens who believe in a pluralistic and tolerant America must not permit the present struggle for the preservation of freedom of conscience to be manipulated into a contest between "humanists" and "liberals" on one side, and evangelical Christians on the other side. This is what the radical right wants. But a religiously crazed and divided America—persecuting its own people on matters of belief and custom—cannot be a force for sanity and moderation in the world.

Indeed, Americans must wake up to the presence of forces that would corrupt our youth and undermine our free institutions. But this threat does not come from a comparatively small number of secular humanists and religious nonconformists. It does not emanate from the American Civil Liberties Union or the Planned Parenthood Association.

The corruptors of youth and the nation come, as so often in the past, from the purveyors of the obscenity of religious intolerance, of reaction parading as the guardian of the American home, of spiritual fascism masquerading as Christianity. Understanding the nature of this challenge and learning how to overcome it is the objective of the chapters that follow.

2

BUILDING THE AUDIENCE:
Evangelicals and the New Right

Americans are a religious people. Very few, including few of the "godless humanists" and "liberals" now attacked by the extreme right, would describe themselves as antireligious, or even as nonreligious.

The influence of religion in our national life is longstanding. When that great foreign observer, Alexis de Tocqueville, landed on the continent 150 years ago, he observed: "The religious atmosphere of the country was the first thing that struck me on arrival in the United States. The longer I stayed in the country, the more conscious I became of the important political consequences resulting from this novel situation."

Upon completing a well-researched survey of American values at the beginning of the 1980s, the Connecticut Mutual Life Insurance Company concluded that "the impact of religious belief . . . has penetrated virtually every dimension of American experience. *This force is rapidly becoming a more powerful factor in American life than whether someone is liberal or conservative, male or female, young or old, or a blue-collar or white-collar worker.*" (Emphasis added.)

The report concluded:

Our findings suggest that the increasing impact of religion on our social and political institutions may be only the beginning of a trend that could change the face of America.

Evidence for growing involvement of morality in politics is abundant. Organized political-religious groups demand that candidates take clear positions on moral issues. They seek to defeat specific candidates who are not considered sufficiently moralistic on selected issues, and even promote single issue candidates for office.

Shortly after his defeat for re-election to the United States Senate in 1980, Senator George McGovern attributed his loss to a saturation campaign by antiabortion forces who successfully labeled McGovern a "baby killer." The defeated senator noted ruefully that their direct-mail and media blitz made the epithet stick, regardless of his effort to explain his position.

Senator Frank Church, defeated in the same election by similar forces, declared: "We have reason to be concerned about the rapid growth of the New Right in such right-wing evangelical movements as the Christian Voice and the Moral Majority." Senator Church, a Presbyterian layman and father of a widely respected Unitarian Universalist minister, found himself, like McGovern, "targeted" for defeat for rejecting the antiabortion amendment, even though Church explained that he and his wife were personally opposed to abortion—a position similar to that taken by President Carter.

Deploring the fanaticism and uncompromising tactics of the extreme Right, Senator Church commented:

The Fundamentalist preachers who occupy the pulpits of the new movement see themselves as the dominant force of the future, destined to determine the nation's political, economic, social and religious agenda. The apparatus they command is commensurate with their ambitions: thirty-six religious TV channels, 1300 religious radio stations, and dozens of gospel TV shows on commercial stations that reach fifty million viewers weekly. In short, the largest media network in the country.

This is what makes the new movement so alarming. Our history is replete with episodes of political intolerance produced

by religious fanaticism, from the days of the Salem witch trials.
But now, in an age of instant mass communication, it is no longer
a single community, but an entire nation that can be victimized.

But what is wrong with having a religious group, whose
members share similar moral values, becoming involved in
public affairs? Is this not an old practice—and one that
liberal and progressive churchmen have used freely?
Senator Church answers:

> The trouble is that the emerging evangelists of the New Right
> are not satisfied with advocacy in a democratic arena, where the
> outcome, favorable or unfavorable, is reached with a measure of
> grace and a reasonable regard for the decency and character of
> those who may disagree.
>
> We are faced, instead, with political evangelists, angry and
> intolerant, incapable of believing that they can be mistaken or
> that those with whom they differ might have honorable inten-
> tions. They see themselves as holders of the absolute truth which
> brooks no opposition. Accordingly, one who does not agree that
> abortion is murder is castigated as a murderer.
>
> In the same manner, those who oppose the restoration of
> school prayer are attacked as atheists; those who support the
> Equal Rights Amendment are branded anti-family, and anyone
> who is against taking sex education out of the curriculum will
> soon find himself portrayed as a moral threat to the community.
>
> In other words, dissenters are devils to be pursued, con-
> demned and exorcized. Clearly, the time has come to remind
> ourselves that the power of the state, once delivered into the
> hands of religious zealots, soon becomes the instrument of
> tyranny.

In the face of a powerful and well-organized force to stir
intolerance, we must wonder whether the influence of religious faith on American life in coming years is to be a force
for understanding and human dignity, or for sectarian warfare
and social strife.

The Connecticut Mutual Life report notes the promise as
well as the danger of rising religious zeal and activism,
especially in light of the finding that Americans are distrust-

ful of recent leadership and impatient for leaders who can inspire.

> The opportunity lies in the opening for a visionary leader to mobilize large numbers of people for national programs of self-sacrifice and devotion to shared goals. The danger lies in the opening for a divisive leader to mobilize large numbers in the service of a partisan campaign to blame the nation's troubles on one group or another labeled "immoral."

It is this circumstance of national frustration and confusion of purpose that the New Right sees as its opportunity to lead. While the inner circle of planners who have charted and organized the right are primarily motivated by secular, economic ideologies and interests, they were quick to recognize the religiously conservative and evangelical masses as an invaluable, perhaps essential, component in their design to build a majority.

Their problem was that evangelical religion, especially its ultraconservative fundamentalist form, had tended to be apolitical. Fundamentalist evangelists preached salvation in the world to come with little attention to the present life, except for the familiar denunciation of sin and worldliness. The faithful were urged to forsake godless civilization, soon to be destroyed in God's coming day of wrath, and to save themselves for life hereafter.

But astute right-wing organizers quickly recognized the growing importance of single issue politics in bringing down liberal and centrist politicians; antigun control, prayer in the schools, opposition to homosexual rights, anti-ERA, and, above all, the antiabortion crusade proved to be graveyard controversies for politicians who collided with the locomotive of single-issue politics.

The New Right's intellectual leaders saw the possibilities for altering the existing alignments of American politics. A vast population, numbering some 25 percent of the nation, was highly responsive to the "moral" issues of sex, family, and patriotism. By and large, they were the less educated, less privileged fourth of the nation. The majority of this target population were white, Protestant or ethnic Catholic, and working class—the "mid-Americans" who during the 1960s and early 70s had displayed increasing resentment at what they perceived as special treatment or "coddling" of racial minorities, women, antiwar youth, homosexuals, and "Communists."

Their religious leaders, especially among Southern and midwestern evangelicals, became increasingly vocal about pornography, drugs, relaxing sexual standards, and the weakening of stable family structures. Godlessness and immorality, fostered by permissive educators and a recently discovered bogeyman—"secular humanism"—provided convenient scapegoats for the stresses and traumas of social dislocation.

Without question, traditionally oriented evangelical and ethnic Catholic cultures found their folkways crumbling. More sophisticated "liberal" populations faced equal or greater stresses and struggled with the tasks of overcoming racism, a morally repugnant conflict in Vietnam, youth alienation, and the dangers of nuclear holocaust.

But the fact that liberals and "humanists" shared the same perplexities of rapid change and social disruption was lost on much of this population. Were drugs out of control? Permissive parents and teachers were to blame. Were marriages breaking down and children dropping out? Experts might be baffled by the human casualties of a technological civilization's exploding complexity—but the electronic preachers had no doubt: Sin and anti-God rebellion were the root causes of our social distress. The willful agents of these evils were "secular" humanists and a decadent, degenerate "liberalism" that provided no moral absolutes.

The sin-hating, humanist-eating electronic evangelists

were ripe for political harvest. Richard Viguerie, the genius of direct mail politics, describes how New Right strategists set about inducting them for combat. Paul Weyrich, director of the Committee for the Survival of a Free Congress, who in Viguerie's estimation symbolizes the best of the New Right, joined forces with Howard Phillips, leader of the Conservative Caucus, and in Viguerie's words "spent countless hours with electronic ministers like Jerry Falwell, Jim Robison, and Pat Robertson, urging them to get involved in conservative politics."

Weyrich would have little trouble finding issues to impress these evangelical men of God. "Paul is constantly looking for new groups to add to the growing New Right coalition," Viguerie writes, "antiabortion groups, veterans groups, religious groups, small businessmen, etc. He believes that family-oriented issues will be the key issues of the 1980's."

Successful religious politics for New Right purposes means the delivery of a large target population, the "most religious" quarter of the nation, most of whom, according to the Connecticut Mutual study cited earlier, are far more likely to vote and to participate in community affairs than less religious (and younger) populations. Falwell, Robison, Pat Robertson, and other right-wing preachers readily responded to the call of Weyrich and Phillips to shepherd this most religious bloc of voters into the rightist alliance.

Whatever the shortcomings of their world view or the limitations of their understanding of biblical theology or anthropology, the fundamentalists are in many respects an exemplary constituency for any party or movement. Franklin D. Roosevelt could not have built his New Deal coalition without these millions of farmers, mill hands, industrial workers, and domestics who loyally followed their beloved chief, even when more affluent and educated constituents threatened to defect.

These groups provided the muscle for peacetime production and the sinews of wartime prowess. They are the people who feed, house, clothe, and transport the nation. They are self-reliant and proud, and quick to take offense when they sense that their values or folkways are being patronized or scorned. The nation's largest "minority," their numbers make them the pivot of political power in America.

We may not admire Weyrich's and Phillips's political calculations or goals, but we can hardly convict them of being stupid. While the two major parties and most political activists played familiar tunes to the usual audiences, New Right ideologues fetched a major constituency. At the time very few even took notice.

If the nation's pundits had been paying closer attention, instead of simply reprocessing each other's received wisdom, we would have recognized the emergence of the evangelicals as a political force in the precipitous rise of Jimmy Carter in the presidential primaries of 1976. The unexpected success and equally swift fall of President Carter can only be explained by this phenomenon.

The usual explanations of Carter's downfall are as unsatisfactory in retrospect as they were uncomprehending in anticipation. Carter's real failure, beyond superficial explanations of "incompetence" and "vacillation," sprang from his inability to hold his original conservative Christian base. He was never favored or accepted by the Democratic establishment. From the outset he was the outsiders' candidate, and when in office Carter showed that his social philosophy was basically mainstream—his personal religious fervor notwithstanding—he was soon abandoned by his early evangelical boosters.

Liberals and mainline Democrats who maintained their preference for other candidates watched Carter sink with little awareness that their fifty-year governing coalition was foundering with him. In fact, many political savants seem still not to realize that Carter's rise in 1976 provided a four-year extension of the moderate coalition's lease on national leadership.

The New Right's political architects have been skillful and shrewd. They have also been lucky. There are many diverse strands and conflicting interests in the fabric of their new conservative coalition, and despite their careful weaving, their alliance may soon begin to fray at the edges.

Contrary to the current identification of "moral" issues with the religious and ideological Right, during much of American history, morality enlisted on the side of humanitarian and progressive causes. The forcible removal of the southeastern Indian tribes in the 1830s was resisted by both liberal and evangelical religious groups as unjust and contrary to the spiritual vision of all people as children of God. The rejection of slavery on moral and religious grounds, beginning with the Quakers and spreading to the evangelical churches—as well as to the unorthodox and theologically liberal Unitarians and Universalists—is a story too familiar to require repetition here. Perhaps less appreciated is the record of the early and determined hostility to slavery of the small farmers of the Piedmont and mountain South. These Calvinist and evangelical rural and highland folk hated the aristocratic planters of the tidewater and organized the southern reaches of the underground railroad that smuggled thousands of fugitive slaves to freedom.

When secession came, the highland countries from Georgia and Alabama northward voted against withdrawal from the Union. Mountain Virginia actually tore asunder from the slave-holding east, gaining admission to the Union as the state of West Virginia. As Appalachian historian and folklorist Donald West has observed, in parts of the mountain South feeling against the Confederacy ran so high that young men slipped to northern lines and volunteered for army service in numbers greater than would have been their quota had they been residents of the North.

Fiercely independent and equalitarian, these evangelical folk defy description as conservative or liberal. Their populist politics is complex. They are as subject as other human beings to holding inconsistent or contradictory opinions without apparent difficulty or embarrassment. They are individualistic and conventional, open to strangers and xenophobic, democratic and despotic, personally generous to a fault and socially parsimonious.

The cipher to unlocking the populist mind is attention to its highly idiosyncratic, moralistic perception of reality. While New Right theologians castigate liberals and humanists for "relativism," few moral perspectives equal the Protestant fundamentalist's resourcefulness in accommodating "God's revealed and unchanging law" to the secular preferences and prejudices of the believer.

Fundamentalist religion rejects systematic theology and philosophy. The Bible is accepted as the only church law, and each believer is admonished to read and interpret for himself, provided the interpretation is literal. The result is a predictable penchant to prove whatever one wishes to prove with an appropriate scriptural text, however far removed the text may be from the question at hand. Fundamentalist theology derives from the method of elevating a few favored biblical passages concerning creation and salvation to total and final authority, while the considerable bulk of biblical literature and history that might cast a different light on religion and ethics is steadfastly ignored, or conveniently "harmonized" with whatever the beholder seeks to maintain.

The inclination to see all moral and religious truth as immediately available to all right-thinking, right-believing people makes it easy for politicians to tap religious prejudice by playing upon instinctive attitudes of moral superiority over novel and unfamiliar life styles and beliefs. The real foundation of fundamentalism is unyielding rural American custom, before which even the meaning of the Bible must conform.

Yet the self-image of the conservative or fundamentalist evangelical remains that of the outsider, the saving remnant rejected by the world and suffering persecution for Christ's sake. To remain unstained of the world is a recurring admonition. One accepts "worldly" honors and power at risk to the soul. The resulting stand-offishness of fundamentalist religion and culture, combined with its recurring proclivity to splinter into sects and factions, has made it a difficult base on which to build a stable political movement. Even so, single issues of a moralistic character—such as Prohibition early in the twentieth century and the antievolution laws of the 1920s—have provided platforms for political careers and national crusades.

But the stubborn individualism of fundamentalist religion has condemned to failure more coherent and comprehensive political agendas. To compound the problem, most highly religious evangelicals and ethnic conservatives are still of the working class. Their economic and social interests are not those of affluent middle-class conservatives. Among this population, liberal leaders like FDR and even populists like Huey Long are remembered far more fondly than William McKinley or Calvin Coolidge.

3

CRITICS WITHIN:
The Contradiction in Rightist
Strategy

Brilliant as their recent electoral strategy may have been, New Right leaders will find their religious partnership a highly volatile and difficult marriage of convenience. A high unemployment rate, or a continued low in housing construction, may loom larger in the mind of bricklayers and roofers than questions of where a political candidate attends church, or whether he or she favors abortion or prayer in school.

A basic contradiction eats at the heart of the "new conservatism." The religious factor makes evident this collision of purposes. Most evangelicals are not ideological zealots, however uncomfortable they may be in a fast moving world that deals roughly with their most cherished institutions and values. They want stability and reassurance, an affirmation of familiar life patterns and inherited values, not new ideological ventures that threaten economic and social benefits they are just beginning to enjoy.

Paul Weyrich, the model "new conservative" of Richard Viguerie's recommendation, illustrates the schism in the conservative philosophy. Weyrich states bluntly: "We are different from previous generations of conservatives. . . . We are radicals, working to overturn the present power structure of the country."

The contradiction imbedded in the effort of the New Right to be both conservative, in the accepted American sense, and "radical" in methods and objectives, is already producing stresses and confrontations.

Senator Barry Goldwater's publically expressed wish to kick the backside of the Reverend Jerry Falwell, which the senator later expanded into a speech condemning the moral arrogance and authoritarianism of the Moral Majority and other New Right preachers, struck many as surprising. Yet, except for the force of Senator Goldwater's expression and candor, there should be nothing unexpected in a statement highlighting the contradiction within the New Right movement. An irrepressible conflict brews within this incompatible marriage of traditional, liberty-loving American individualism—the essence of the "old" conservatism—and the authoritarianism and coerciveness of twentieth-century right-wing radicalism.

The New Right seeks to exploit the popular desire to "get the government off our backs and out of our lives." But how do they propose to achieve this objective? By abridging the First Amendment to mandate state-sponsored "voluntary" prayer in public education, by amending the Constitution to overturn the right to privacy upheld by the Supreme Court with respect to abortion, by writing legislation to restrict the power of the courts to review violations of civil liberties, by abrogating limits on state power to inquire into consensual sexual relationships between adults, through legislation to ferret out homosexuals and to prescribe private sexual conduct, and by saddling taxpayers with a heavy increase in armaments to "roll back" communism.

The New Right holds almost as a religious dogma the expectation of Soviet aggression and, with that expectation, makes a demand for a militarily superior America. In contrast, the old conservatives feared militarism and the drift toward a garrison state.

The religious right's peculiar notion of preserving freedom by attacking traditional liberties is expressed in the torrent of abuse directed against every tendency in American life that can even remotely be described as humanistic, liberal, or nonconformist.

The New Right's intrusion of state power into every facet of personal life is the antithesis of traditional American conservatism, which shared with Jeffersonian liberalism a profound respect for constitutional liberties and privacy of conscience. It is, therefore, hardly any wonder that a veteran conservative such as Senator Goldwater objects to this crusade against personal moral freedom masquerading as conservatism.

If Barry Goldwater refused to accept the Moral Majority as a conservative movement, Billy Graham has similar problems in equating its political agenda with Christianity. Shortly after the 1980 elections Graham remarked: "The hard right has no interest in religion except to manipulate it. . . . I told [Falwell] to preach the gospel. That's our calling. I want to preserve the purity of the gospel and the freedom of religion in America." Making clear that he finds the New Right's holy war against liberalism and humanism religiously defective and morally offensive Dr. Graham declared: "I don't want to see religious bigotry in any form."

Billy Graham is a Southern Baptist, although like many evangelical leaders he has never emphasized denominational structures and urges converts at his revivals to join any evangelical or orthodox Christian church of their choice. Early in his career, Graham condemned the United Nations and supporters of what he dubbed a "one world" philosophy —to the gratification of his early patron, William Randolph Hearst. But as Billy Graham matured and saw more of the world, eventually preaching behind the Iron Curtain, he broadened his perspective. Widely recognized as the most influential preacher of our time, Graham can serve today as the embodiment of the changes that have overtaken a generation of evangelicals. To understand why Falwell and the ideologues who recruited him are likely to fail in their drive to organize a permanent evangelical voting bloc we should look more closely at Billy Graham and the millions who respond to his message.

Some years ago when the issue of racial segregation was sundering churches in the South, Graham announced that henceforth there would be no racially segregated seating at his Crusades for Christ. Every man or woman was equal before Christ, he insisted. Graham's personal influence was such that his decision stuck.

Without question, had Graham announced such a policy at the beginning of his career, or perhaps only a few years earlier than he did, the world probably would have heard little of Billy Graham. Yet, having taken his step when conceivably it could have seriously split his following, Graham turned a corner in his public career. No longer could he be dismissed by thoughtful critics as simply a country bumpkin or a mere religious huckster—an assessment that had dogged his early career. Many among the clergy had earlier shrugged Graham off as a superficial preacher whose only distinction was a loud voice and a primitive view of this world and the next.

While his impassioned declamatory style is not to everyone's taste, there is no question that Graham has few peers as a popular orator, having the gift to transfix multitudes in the difficult setting of open air mass rallies. Hitler and Mussolini could move throngs for an evil end. Martin Luther King could do it with equal mastery for a good purpose. But few others in our lifetime are in Graham's league in the ability to hold audiences, drawing each listener into rapt one-to-one confrontation with the evangelist's urgent message.

Seldom profound, too frequently glib, and susceptible to

the cocksureness of the convinced, Graham has his limitations as a teacher and thinker. But his sincerity and personal
integrity have won general respect even among those who
reject his theology. Frequenting the Nixon White House as a
guest on display, Graham learned the hard way the price of
political co-optation and vowed not to repeat his mistake.

Working-class evangelicals identify with Graham and his
message because he represents their class, culture, and
fervent faith. Trained for the ministry at fundamentalist
colleges and seminaries of the South and Midwest, where
many youth of modest circumstances and limited educational
opportunities prepare for their calling, William Franklin
Graham began his career as pastor of a Baptist church in
Illinois before becoming a full-time evangelist.

Graham's personal religious experience began with the
familiar evangelical conviction of being a lost sinner called to
repentance by the saving voice of Christ. In the language of
evangelicals, Graham became "twice-born," emerging from
his spiritual experience as a new being "washed in the blood
of the Lamb." This is standard evangelical doctrine, having
its foundation in the New Testament letters of St. Paul, where
Christian doctrine first achieves systematic expression.

Evangelical Protestantism makes this conversion experience the essential center of religious life. Rituals, churchly
creeds, and systematic theologies occupy a secondary position. Strict evangelicals teach that without this personal
rebirth in Christ as the only intercessor between God and the
human soul, there can be no salvation either in this world or
the world to come. These evangelicals insist that such
teachings must be accepted literally. There is nothing
metaphorical or imaginary about the afterlife; the joys of
heaven and pains of hell are real, and endless. It follows from
this conception of human destiny that for true Christians
redeeming souls is the most important work on earth. That
mission must dominate every aspect of the evangelical

Christian's life. While this belief easily lends itself to contempt for other faiths, the "great commission" that orthodox Christians believe Christ gave to his disciples to save souls leads principled evangelicals to reject intimidation or coercion, including the ministrations of the state.

The deep spiritual foundation of evangelical Christian faith, as well as unwavering commitment to liberty of conscience, can be seen in the historic "Statement of Baptist Faith and Message" of the Southern Baptist Convention. Adopted in 1925 amid the heat of the evolution controversy and with acrimony between fundamentalists and modernists dividing churches, the statement reflects centuries of Baptist experience and comes as close as Baptists can to a creed. Its article on religious liberty states:

> God alone is Lord of the conscience, and he has left it free from the doctrines and commandments of men which are contrary to his word or not contained in it. Church and state should be separate. The state owes to the church protection and full freedom in the pursuit of its spiritual ends. In providing such freedom no ecclesiastical group or denomination should be favored by the state more than others. Civil government being ordained of God, it is the duty of Christians to render loyal obedience thereto in all things not contrary to the revealed word of God. The church should not resort to the civil power to carry on its work. The Gospel of Christ contemplates spiritual means alone for the pursuit of its ends. The state has no right to impose penalties for religious opinions of any kind. The state has no right to impose taxes for the support of any form of religion. A free church in a free state is the Christian ideal, and this implies the right of free and unhindered access to God on the part of all men. and the right to form and propagate opinions in the sphere of religion without interference by the civil power.

What Billy Graham recognizes—and what the Falwells, Robisons, and Robertsons have yet to learn from their own tradition of spiritual liberty—is that if your aim is to lead "erring souls" to salvation, whether they be Jews, humanists, or "unregenerate" Christians, you cannot do so by coercing or persecuting them. You may not be successful in your mission whatever you do, but you cannot love your neighbors "in Christ" and preach contempt and intolerance for them at the same time.

When the current president of the Southern Baptist Convention was imprudent enough to say that God does not hear the prayer of a Jew—a reasonable assumption by his lights, since Jews, like other non-Christians, do not call upon God in the name of Christ the "intercessor"—other evangelicals, including Southern Baptist theologians, suggested he leave that determination to God. Bailey Smith later apologized to the Jewish community, stating that he had made a mistake in singling out Jews in making his point that all souls must approach God the Father only through Christ. Later when he and a group of Baptists visited Israel on a good-will mission arranged by B'nai B'rith, Israeli religious leaders concluded that Smith was sincere, even if parochial in his experience, and that he had attempted to make a theological rather than an anti-Semitic statement.

Billy Graham's Baptists constitute nearly half of all evangelical Protestants in the United States; their pattern of organization, which is typical of many other evangelical sects, illustrates the practical impossibility of achieving uniformity of belief or action for any purpose, religious or political. Many Baptists glory in this multiplicity, viewing it as the consequence as well as the guarantee of their great historic principle of "soul freedom."

The problem of capturing such a diverse and tumultuous religious culture is obvious from its very composition. Strictly speaking, there is no such thing as "the Baptist church," only local, self-governing churches—scores of thousands of such congregations—loosely organized into some twenty different associations or conventions. The Southern Baptist Convention, the largest, with 35,000 congregations and 13 million members, contains almost half of all Baptists in the United States. Its growing member churches can now be found both north and south, although its southern base still provides the bulk of its strength and assures its prevailing conservative-to-fundamentalist theology. Ironically, several thousand congregations have withdrawn from the convention, finding its doctrines too "liberal" to meet their strict literalist interpretation of scripture.

There are numerous other varieties of Baptist. The old Northern Baptist Convention, now titled the American Baptist Churches in the U.S.A., is the most liberal and "modernist" in theology and social philosophy. Its leaders have included such distinguished figures as Harry Emerson Fosdick and the liberal gadfly and activist Harvey Cox. This racially integrated body of 1,500,000 members is also represented throughout the United States.

Collectively the several large black Baptist conventions approach in numbers the predominantly white Southern Baptists. In addition, there are thousands of independent congregations, ranging from tiny store fronts to booming tabernacles with many thousands of members. (Jerry Falwell claims more than 16,000 for his independent Thomas Road Baptist Church in Lynchburg, Virginia.)

Many Baptists have a strong tradition of social conscience and economic justice. In New York City nearly a century ago, a Baptist preacher and theologian, Walter Rauschenbusch, became a leading figure in the Social Gospel movement, a liberal, humanitarian movement among Protestant churches that stressed an ethical interpretation of Christianity as a call for social and economic justice. The Social Gospel has declined as a movement, its liberal theology rejected as too optimistic, but its influence continues in the active social witness of the churches, a commitment to human well-being that many believers see as a necessary aspect of their religion, if not its very heart.

Noting that the Moral Majority represents a departure from the historic attachment of Baptists to religious freedom, and the privacy of conscience on such issues as abortion and prayer in the school, Dr. Carl Flemister, Executive Minister of the American Baptist Churches of Metropolitan New York remarks:

> The electronic pulpiteers are seeking to shape the American republic into their vision of a Christian utopia. They proclaim a righteous nation which is pro-family, pro-free market enterprise, anti-abortion, anti-alternate life-style and anti-feminist.
>
> The New Right stands at the ready, battering rams aimed at the wall of separation. Their intent: the formation of an American-Christian republic.
>
> What a travesty! What a betrayal of the pluralistic possibilities of this great nation!

Declaring a different vision of the relationship between society and faith from the one preached by the religious right, Flemister goes on to assert:

> Baptists have been very much concerned about public issues and the conduct of state. But we have acted as citizens who are Baptists and not as Baptists who would shape the state in our own image. For that to happen would be a fundamental contradiction for any Baptist—Jerry Falwell included.

Flemister sees the New Right foundering in its effort to capture America's thirty million Baptists and an equal number of evangelicals in other like-minded denominations. "Two doctrines are very clear to Baptists and are important to the crisis of our time—the doctrine of individual freedom of conscience and the doctrine of separation of church and state."

Insert the name of almost any other evangelical sect wherever Carl Flemister says Baptist, and you will find the position of the majority of religious people in America.

What light does this glimpse into evangelical organization

and doctrine cast upon Jerry Falwell's Moral Majority or the ideological designs of the New Right? It means, in the judgment of many evangelical theologians, that the politicized fundamentalism of the New Right is a heresy. It perverts the gospel to a worldly purpose and violates the Pauline injunction to "be all things to all men" in order to serve the cause of bringing souls to Christ. Paul was not advising duplicity, as a modern reading of his words might imply. He was urging the true follower of the gospel not to violate the personality of others, to reach out on the basis of empathy and understanding of the nonbeliever's experience and moral awareness.

Many observers believe that evangelical Christians who are well grounded in their religion are not likely to be co-opted by the radical right, or by any other authoritarian political or economic movement. To do so would be to subordinate and deflect the purpose of their faith. When Billy Graham said of Jerry Falwell: "I told him to preach the gospel. That is our calling," Graham was perhaps pronouncing a prophecy of the ultimate failure of the New Right's effort to suborn religion for political ends.

But as prophetic as that may be for the future, the religious right has today assembled a formidable, often militant minority with a demonstrated ability to swing elections, shake legislators, and harass school boards.

4

THE TARGETS AND THE ATTACKERS:

The Politics of Intolerance

"When the U.S. Supreme Court prohibited children from participating in voluntary prayers in public schools, the conclusion is inescapable that the Supreme Court not only violated the right of free exercise of religion for all Americans; it also established a national religion in the United States—the religion of secular humanism." So writes Senator Jesse Helms in his introduction to evangelist Homer Duncan's book *Secular Humanism: The Most Dangerous Religion in America.*

This "national religion" is the same "Satanic philosophy" diagnosed by television evangelist James Robison as "one of the great cancers eating away the heart of our once great nation."

Argues Dr. Tim La Haye, California spokesman for the Moral Majority: "Humanism is a fiendishly evil religion that damns not only the soul, but also the present life."

"As Secular Humanism takes a more pessimistic outlook toward man's progress, humanists look more to the State to assume a guiding hand in shaping man's future," Duncan quotes John W. Whitehead and John Conlan as writing in the *Texas Tech Law Review*. They assert that "because man does not seem to be progressing in the evolutionary sense, many Secular Humanists have opted for forced progress and manipulative environment control. Totalitarianism, therefore, could very well be the end result of Secular Humanism."

And Duncan invites us: "In the event that you feel these writers have been unjust in their presentation of the beliefs of Secular Humanism, read Humanist Manifesto I and II."

Joe McCarthy would be proud! Old Joe liked to describe innocuous documents in hair-raising terms, knowing that, unless challenged, few of his audience would question "the evidence I hold in my hand." Like McCarthy, Duncan recognizes that few readers of his Missionary Crusader publications are likely to read either humanist statement, and the slurs on his victims will be accepted as just.

The use of wild generalization, guilt by association—mere description by a label like "liberal," "modernist," "secular," "humanist," or any combination thereof will do—and outright fabrication of the victims' beliefs and attitudes is fair game for the witch hunters of the "hard right." It is easy enough to accuse humanists of subscribing to opposite evils at the same time. Strong historic attachment to a civil libertarian emphasis on personal freedom and individual rights makes humanists guilty of "moral relativism" and of "weakening" moral standards necessary for "public decency"; at the same time advocacy by humanists of legislation to protect the disadvantaged and to conserve the environment becomes evidence of "statism" and "a drift to totalitarianism."

In these pages we shall act upon evangelist Duncan's advice to go to the source to examine for ourselves what humanists believe about democracy, the limits of state power, and individual rights. But what humanists may believe is less important to right-wing propagandists than their usefulness as living embodiments of evil. Liberals and "modernists" in general are agents of decadence and corruption; but "secular humanists" embody most fully the ethos of a contemporary society that the Christian far right distrusts and would like to exorcize. Partisans of the radical right who may not be religious themselves find these popular misconceptions and fears politically useful and exploit them to the fullest.

All agents of Satan take on the same aspect in this "humanist" house of horrors. Thus, Bertrand Russell, a respected figure in the history of liberal thought, is likened to Lenin and Stalin, whom Russell despised for their brutality and tyranny; but Russell, like the Bolshevik leaders, was an "atheist," and therefore qualifies as a vintage bogeyman. Hitler, the supreme example of right-wing totalitarianism in our time, curiously becomes a "humanist" in religious right literature, for no obvious reason except his standing as a certified monster. The fact that the Nazi leader persecuted humanists and liberals and believed himself chosen by Providence to fulfill Aryan destiny is passed over in silence.

As we saw earlier, support for abortion rights or opposition to prayer in the public school is sufficient to qualify an opponent as a "godless" liberal and/or humanist. Such abuse of words having a constructive and honored history can serve no purpose except paralysis of thought.

Probably no one would have heard of the "religion of secular humanism" except for a footnote in Justice Black's opinion in the Torcaso case of 1961, in which an atheist in Maryland was upheld by the Supreme Court in his right to qualify as a notary public. In delivering the unanimous opinion of the Court, Justice Black noted: "Among religions in this country which do not teach what would generally be considered a belief in God are Buddhism, Taoism, Ethical Culture, Secular Humanism and others." At the time, this choice of labels was considered odd by humanists themselves, since among humanists "secular" and "religious" are usually used to describe two contrasting approaches to humanism.

The secular humanist would ordinarily resist classifying humanism as a religion. In contrast, those adhering to humanism as a religious philosophy would be inclined to avoid describing themselves as "secular humanists," rejecting the adjective in this context as misleading. (The most likely explanation of Justice Black's choice of terminology is stylistic, an effort on his part to avoid the awkwardness of using the adjective "religious" to describe the noun "religion.")

Whatever may have been in the jurist's mind, his choice of language has led to endless controversy about the standing of humanism in law and society. Is every secular aspect of humanistic thought to be treated now as religious in the constitutional sense?

The confusion is popular, not profoundly legal. The same term obviously may apply to more than one idea or interest. The word liberal, for example, has one meaning in theology, quite another in economics—in fact, two opposite meanings—and yet another in morals. Similarly, the inclusive conception of humanism, enriched and elaborated over the centuries, has taken on a multiplicity of applications. The common denominator of all these usages, these various "humanisms," is attachment to the significance of the human venture on earth and a high estimate of the worth and dignity of human life, quite apart from theological or other-worldly considerations. This meaning of humanism has held steady since the Renaissance. In this construction, and this construction only, all humanisms including religious humanism are "secular," all treating this life as inherently interesting, creative, and worthwhile as an end in itself.

But from this point of similarity the various humanisms and "humanistic" arts and sciences diverge widely. They range from the interpretation of religion as a nonsupernatural human phenomenon to the practical applications of physics to human survival and well-being.

Thanks to the Court's use of terms in *Torcaso*, religious humanism, which had lead a quiet existence for most of the past hundred years as a school of thought principally within liberal Unitarian and Universalist churches and Ethical Culture societies, was suddenly recognized by the extreme right as the scourge of American life, the source of the drug culture, youth rebellion, permissiveness, sexual license, and the general breakdown of morality and social discipline. It matters little that students of American cultural history have generally acknowledged the many social, intellectual, and ethical contributions of these numerically small bodies of religious liberals.

Unlike more traditional philosophies of religion, those who designate themselves as religious humanists shift the emphasis from a God-centered faith to a this-worldly religion of applied ethics and human development. When shortly after the American Civil War a young Reform rabbi conceived the idea of a new type of religious community based exclusively on the cultivation of ethical relationships without necessary reference to ritual or a doctrine of God, he coined the term "ethical culture." Although not explicitly humanist in its origin, Felix Adler's Society for Ethical Culture helped set the pattern for future "humanist" and "liberal religious" congregations, including many churches of the now merged Unitarian Universalist faith, which, while retaining their historic identity evolved into nontheistic religious societies based on humanism. (Many other Unitarian Universalist congregations continue to maintain a more traditional God-centered philosophy, and virtually all respect individual freedom in matters of belief.)

Pioneer religious humanists and Ethical Culturists offered no special revelation or occult truth. On the contrary, their purpose was to reconceive religious thought in terms of the findings of modern science and philosophy. Standing at the opposite end of the spectrum from ultraorthodox and fundamentalist types of faith, they stressed the place of reason and the use of the scientific method in arriving at a more adequate understanding of the universe and the place of human life within it. The Bible continued to be respected as a source of ancient wisdom but lost its position as the revealed word of God.

Some early humanistic theologians and philosophers attempted to reinterpret the historic doctrines of Judaism and Christianity in line with contemporary thinking. Others felt that such an approach was timid and compromising, calling instead for frank recognition that no theology or world view can be regarded as valid for all time. Jewish and Christian monotheism represented a historic advance beyond animism and pagan polytheism, but the theistic-supernaturalist world view would itself be superseded by a naturalistic world view, a conception of reality that does not assume a divine first cause. Religious humanists held a variety of views on the God question, some taking an agnostic position of suspended judgment, some declaring frankly for atheism, and others insisting that theological concepts were necessarily conjectural or unanswerable. Therefore, they argued, theological controversy should be laid aside as an unprofitable speculation; instead, morality and religious commitment should be based upon inner sanctions derived from human need and aspiration. This "nontheistic" position (in contrast to atheism, which remains locked in dispute about the existence of God) regards theological argumentation as futile and a diversion of energy from the serious life-nurturing task of ethical, humanistic living.

This obviously is not a religious philosophy designed for mass appeal in a culture deeply steeped in evangelical, orthodox Christian theism. Nevertheless, the religion of humanism has provided spiritual anchorage for many thousands of serious-minded Americans who retain a religious feeling about life and appreciate some expression of religious community and commitment, but who no longer find themselves intellectually comfortable within the traditional creeds. A century of history seems to indicate that the appeal of humanism will remain limited to a small segment of the religious population, even though it may continue to play a seminal part in the advancement of moral and religious thought.

Why, given this minor place, do right-wing fundamentalists make a devil out of a type of religious expression that barely touches their world?

The answer appears to be two-fold: (1) Right-wing demagogues need a witch to burn for the gratification of the faithful, and (2) they find it useful to confuse the religion of humanism, a minor affair as they clearly know, with the all-pervasive influence of the philosophy of science and the intellectual impact of secular democratic thought. A school of religious philosophy that accepts both the scientific world view and a secular democratic conception of society offers an irresistible temptation to right-wing fundamentalists to turn history on its head and contend that science and secular democracy are products of "the religion of secular humanism." We have already shown the fallacy of this cart-before-the-horse argument.

As a general perspective on life and nature, humanism is not so much a specific philosophy as the general spirit of modern Western civilization. Who is not a humanist in one aspect or another of thought and action? A mere listing of the applications of the humanistic approach to the arts and sciences reads like an encyclopedia of intellectual and social life: humanistic education, humanistic psychology, humanistic anthropology and sociology, humanistic ethics, the humanistic uses of science, etc.

By humanistic psychology, for example, the late Abraham

Maslow sought to establish a "third force" in the science of psychology, that would be distinct from both orthodox Freudianism and "reductionist behaviorism." In political economy, social democrat Erich Fromm proposed the term "humanistic socialism" to stand in contrast to the dehumanized authoritarianism and dictatorship of Soviet Communism. Fromm also conceived of "humanistic democracy" as a democratic culture in which the human qualities would flourish, unlike the impersonal structures of mass culture that kill the spirit and remain democratic in form only.

These many applications of the humanistic *zeitgeist* demonstrate the impossibility of linking the educational humanism of the schools, the psychological humanism of the mental health clinic, or the social humanism of the services agency to the religious humanism of the liberal churches or the more "secular" humanism of the American Humanist Association and various other freethought and rationalist groups. There is a common element in each of these applications of the humanistic "spirit," but that element, far from being the property of an exclusive philosophical party or sect, is the intellectual and moral cement that binds together Western democratic civilization—at base a belief in human beings and their dignity.

Ignoring these distinctions, the religious New Right continues to whip up a state of popular hysteria against an effigy of their own creation, "the religion of secular humanism" that a diabolical Supreme Court has "established" as the godless "national religion" of the United States.

The attack on religious humanism (or "the religion of secular humanism," to invoke the sinister-sounding phrase favored by rightist orators) is one of the most explicit and best organized campaigns in American history to promote bigotry against a religious minority for political and ideological ends. Fortunately, it is unlikely to result in the personal damage brought about by other efforts to whip up religious prejudice, such as anti-Semitism. Most religious humanists are solidly established members of the white gentile middle class, well educated and otherwise indistinguishable from their neighbors. Most are self-confident individualists who are more likely to be amused than frightened by the right-wing smoke and fury unleashed against them. Nevertheless, there are others living in isolated and backward communities whose views may lead to social reprisal, job discrimination, or even dismissal. Being a conspicuous religious nonconformist in a conservative Texas town, for example, is not likely to advance one's career as a public school teacher or community leader. Yet, the number of individuals so affected is likely to be small, because of the relative security and social position of most humanists.

The major risk is to American public opinion and to the "moral majority" itself. Many unsophisticated people, who traditionally respect and trust their religious leaders, may fall victim to the distortions and outright falsifications of a new breed of preachers of hate. When a United States Senator drapes the mantle of Christian piety around his shoulders and encourages a witch hunt against "secular humanism," why shouldn't ordinary people believe the danger to be imminent?

Homer Duncan, taking full advantage of his senatorial endorsement, improves on Falwell's "humanism is Communism" by providing seemingly credible elaboration: "Humanism and Communism are not identical twins," he soberly tells us, "but they are good bedfellows. Communism is humanism in political disguise." He argues that "a comparison of the Communist Manifesto with Humanist Manifestos I and II reveals that their aims are almost identical." When we wonder in what ways these diametrically opposite social philosophies can be alike, he tells us that "both seek the betterment of the human race."

This extraordinary "accusation"—seeking human betterment—is one that probably even the most conservative humanist would not care to refute. It is coupled with more serious (and false) representations of humanism as a movement with dictatorial designs. Humanists are described as seeking "to destroy all religions, except their own." Equally far-fetched is the charge that an alleged humanist goal is "to control the educational system."

"Humanism is Communism," a refrain of the religious right, usually falls back on vague references to two historic summaries of humanist belief, the Humanist Manifesto of 1933 and the Second Human Manifesto of 1973. As described elsewhere in this volume, neither statement speaks with authority for any organization; both are consensus statements of individual signers. Neither claims to represent final truth or the sum total of humanist thought. Both are working papers, subject to amendment. And both affirm democracy and human freedom. Apparently it is the word "Manifesto" that provides a very tempting target for the religious right. To their minds Manifesto can mean only a Communist document. Thus, while humanist organizations and individuals have issued hundreds of statements over the years, Humanist Manifestos I and II receive most of the attention from the right.

Since the present writer was not only a signer of Humanist Manifesto II, but also served on the committee that drafted it, I can speak with some authority about the thinking and motives of those who composed the document. My part in framing the Manifesto was modest, limited to reviewing proposed drafts and making suggestions, and I have no personal investment in its style or emphasis. It is primarily the work of Paul Kurtz, professor of philosophy, the State University of New York at Buffalo, and at that time editor of the *Humanist* magazine; assisted by Roy Fairfield, an associate editor of the *Humanist* and professor of education at Antioch College. My colleague on the Board of Leaders of the New York Society for Ethical Culture and also associate editor of the *Humanist*, Khoren Arisian (who has since returned to the Unitarian Universalist ministry), was among the other members of the drafting committee.

There was not a single participant in the entire editorial group whose political views could remotely be described as far left. A primary purpose of the document, in fact, was to underscore humanism's commitment to individual freedom and the democratic process. The only Soviet signer was the humanist and liberal Andrei Sakarov, whose signature on such a "bourgeois" declaration was an act of courage.

At the time of the Manifesto we all shared an anxiety about the revolutionary rhetoric of "radical" student groups during the period prior to 1973, the increasing alienation of many young people from American democracy, and their frank cynicism that constitutional methods were effective or relevant. Minor but disturbing cults of violent action had arisen, exemplified in their most overt form by the Weather Underground and the Black Liberation Army. Such extremism on the left could only produce its opposite, a more than equal reaction from fanatics on the right. For every potential Weatherman in America there are a thousand prospective Klansmen. The great moral gains of the nonviolent Civil Rights movement and courageous moral resistance to an indefensible war were being squandered by the nihilism of a handful—which, with their proclivity to follow fads, many youth were mindlessly imitating.

There is no question that the overwhelming majority of those in the civil rights and peace movement were moved by idealistic and democratic principles. We had put much of ourselves into those struggles. But the media, by constantly focusing their cameras on small disciplined bands of disrupters, shouting hate for America and flaunting their revolutionary banners, helped to create the specter of an army of rebels grinding their heritage underfoot. Those viewing from afar, unable to discount the sensationalism of the media, could only conclude that powerful forces of subversion were at large, that "outside agitators," as racial and political bigots had been insisting, were behind the movements for social justice and peace.

As humanists, both religious and nonreligious humanists, we had an obligation to throw the full weight of our influence in support of constitutional, democratic methods and standards. Humanist Manifesto II emerged as an unqualified affirmation of democracy and a sharp rebuke to covert, authoritarian means of effecting social change.

James Robison, a television preacher who ritualistically assails humanism as "this Satanic philosophy," refrains from quoting the text of Humanist Manifesto II on the dignity of the person and the necessity for free, democratic government:

> The preciousness and dignity of the individual person is a central humanistic value. Individuals should be encouraged to realize their own creative talents and desires. We reject all religions, ideological, or moral codes that denigrate the individual, suppress freedom, dull intellect, dehumanize personality. We believe in maximum individual autonomy consonant with social responsibility.

This traditional American emphasis on personal worth and individual rights, the very essence of the philosophy of ethical humanism, is reinforced by a commitment to support and expand the personal freedoms assured in the Bill of Rights.

> To enhance freedom and dignity the individual must experience a full range of *civil liberties* in all societies. This includes freedom of speech and the press, political democracy, the legal right of opposition to governmental policies, fair judicial process, religious liberty, freedom of association, and artistic, scientific, and cultural freedom.

The declaration takes note of the development of authoritarian methods of control and expresses opposition to the increasing invasion of privacy, by whatever means in both totalitarian and democratic societies. We would safeguard, extend, and implement the principles of human freedom evolved from the *Magna Carta* to the *Bill of Rights*, the *Rights of Man*, and the *Universal Declaration of Human Rights*.

This emphatic and specific declaration of loyalty to a heritage of nearly a thousand years is passed over in silence by right-wing ideologues who persist in treating the Manifesto as a "Communist" document.

Humanist Manifesto II is not a perfect statement. Like the platform of a diverse national political party, it rambles and tends to include "something for everyone." But despite its deficiencies, the Manifesto is a forceful affirmation of democracy and constitutional government within the American tradition of individual rights, an open political process, and the limitation of state power.

The very scope and variety of humanist thought in the modern world makes it an easy target for demagogues to find something to attack. If Alexander Dubcek and his circle of reformers in the Czechoslovakian government and party could speak approvingly of "socialism with a human face," before Soviet tanks ended their brief experiment, that is enough evidence for right-wingers to make their simplistic deduction: If Marxists can appeal to humanistic ideals, then humanists must be Marxists. And Marxists must be Leninists and Stalinists and Maoists, "waiting in the wings" to come to power.

The diversity and richness of the humanist tradition may be seen in this excerpt from Humanist Manifesto II itself:

Many kinds of humanism exist in the contemporary world. The varieties and emphases of naturalistic humanism include "scientific," "ethical," "democratic," "religious," and "Marxist" humanism. Free thought, atheism, agnosticism, skepticism, deism, rationalism, ethical culture, and liberal religion all claim to be heir to the humanist tradition. Humanism traces its roots from ancient China, classical Greece and Rome, through the

Renaissance and the Enlightenment, to the scientific revolution of the modern world. . . . Humanism is an ethical process through which we can all move, above and beyond the divisive particulars. . . .

The umbrella is as broad as the liberating and democratizing elements of Western civilization, and of parallel currents in Oriental and other cultures as well. Under this umbrella exist many competing tendencies and viewpoints. But the sum of this diversity is not the spiritual chaos and moral anarchy that the ideological far right supposes. Nor is there any tendency toward totalitarian control. The common denominator is high regard for, and commitment to human dignity and personal rights within an open, democratic society where no orthodoxy can silence reason and no majority is permitted to stifle dissent.

5

SEX AS A POLITICAL WEAPON:
Abortion, Homosexuality, and
Theocratic Law

The New Right recognized the potential of religious politics in achieving a conservative majority when Paul Weyrich and his associates recruited Jerry Falwell and other evangelists to work in support of right-wing "moral" causes.

"Paul Weyrich is very optimistic about the future impact of the pro-family movement," writes Richard Viguerie in *The New Right: We're Ready to Lead,* attributing to Weyrich the opinion that "family issues in the 1980's could be what Vietnam was in the 1960's and environmental and consumer issues were in the 1970's for the left."

At the center of the "pro-family" movement is a group of organizations that can hardly compete with the Moral Majority as a household word, yet that in Viguerie's estimate "has enormous political strength." Taking its name from the short street on Capitol Hill where it was first organized, the "Library Court" coalition by 1980 had grown to include some twenty organizations representing millions of members.

"In sheer numbers," Viguerie quotes Weyrich as saying, "the potential outreach of the Library Court group is greater than the whole range of conservative groups." It brings into alliance for political action such bodies as the Christian Coalition for Legislative Action, the Moral Majority, the American Association for Christian Schools, Citizens for Educational Freedom, the American Life Lobby, Conservatives Against Liberal Legislation, Family America, and the Conservative Caucus Research, Analysis and Education Foundation.

The alliance got off to a flying start in 1979, according to Viguerie, by organizing "a flood of mail" to thwart plans of the Department of Health, Education, and Welfare to sponsor research on "test-tube" babies. It may seen ironic that a "pro-life, pro-family" coalition would undertake as their opening effort a campaign to halt fertility research to make child-bearing possible for otherwise sterile couples.

But it is no more ironic than other "Library Court" manifestations of "support" for mothers and children. Many of their stands have taken legislative form in Senator Laxalt's Family Protection Bill. This omnibus measure covers the spectrum of conservative "pro-life" and "pro-family" proposals, including a ban on governmental "intrusion" into such private matters as a husband's freedom to beat his wife! (The same mentality in the recent past has blocked government funding of day-care centers for the children of working mothers on the argument that mothers should be "encouraged" to stay at home with their children.)

Other features of the proposed Family Protection Act include denial of Federal aid-to-education funds to states that do not permit prayer in public buildings, denial of funds for textbooks that fail to support the traditional image of the role of women, and a provision forbidding the use of funds by the Legal Services Corporation to support abortion cases, litigation on behalf of school desegregation, legal aid for divorce, or to challenge discrimination against homosexuals. Many other antireform and antiliberal provisions are included in this fifty-page bill in the guise of upholding the traditional roles of men and women and strengthening the family.

Viguerie describes a luncheon hosted by Senator Lexalt for "the nation's top evangelical leaders" who "promised an all-out effort" in support of his legislative proposal. Laxalt declared that "for years we have been debating on the terms of those who want to remake society. Now those groups *will have to explain* [emphasis added] why they oppose the traditional idea of the family."

The labels "pro-life" and "pro-family" have become so elastic as to include any measure which the political right can sell to their religious allies on the pretext of preserving traditional American values. Some are so far-fetched as to appear utterly unreal. Religious freedom becomes a slogan for exempting private "Christian academies" from civil rights compliance or adherence to state-mandated educational standards. The padlocked Christian school is invoked as the horrifying spectacle of godless persecution to come, as organizers of church-run basement schools defy state efforts to enforce compliance with laws that other citizens are obliged to obey.

Abortion, free sex, homosexuality, and pornography are touted as the principal battlegrounds, staked out by the religious right in their war against pluralistic, "liberal" society. That liberals, feminists, and humanists were critics of the debasing commercialization of sex long before rightists moved to monopolize the issue for themselves is conveniently forgotten. Because the authoritarian right is far less sensitive to the constitutional problems of censorship and the right to privacy, rightists can easily upstage their opposition depicting them as "amoral" and even as conspiring to undermine the family and promote promiscuity.

The political exploitation of sex-related issues did more than give the nonreligiously motivated New Right a bridge on which to reach the fundamentalist masses. It also provided a common ground upon which to link two traditionally suspicious and hostile antagonists: conservative evangelical Protestants and conservative Roman Catholics.

Conservative Protestant leaders had shown scant interest in abortion until recently. Abortion was regarded as a Catholic issue, somewhat extended from traditional Catholic opposition to birth control. The Supreme Court's abortion rights decision appealed to many conservative Protestants' traditional respect for personal privacy and the limitation of government snooping.

But while evangelical and fundamentalist churchmen concerned themselves with other matters, leaving "the right to life" movement largely to the Catholic bishops and their followers, homosexual rights jumped into prominence with growing public acceptance of homosexuals as members of the community. The movement for homosexual rights obviously followed in the wake of the movement for women's rights, which in turn had followed the civil rights movement for racial equality.

Each of these movements to gain equality for a disadvantaged group nettled white religious conservatives, who by and large accepted the myth of racial separation and black dependence as "God's law" and saw the traditional relations of the sexes as divinely mandated. Traditional Catholics and Protestants (and orthodox Jews) could agree that homosexuality was "an abomination in the eyes of the Lord." The more relaxed sexual standards that followed improved contraception and women's liberation posed an additional moral crisis for all social and religious traditionalists.

With television personality Anita Bryant leading as the personification of the movement, the counterattack against public acceptance of homosexuality began. It was a cause in which Southern fundamentalist Protestants could show unreserved feeling, demonstrating as passionately for "decency" and "family protection" as militant Catholics were crusading against "baby killers" and a prenatal "holocaust." Each group of zealots discovered the other. People who had enthusiastically hated each other for four centuries, and whose cousins still slaughter one another in Northern Ireland, found they could agree to find others to hate—sexually emancipated women, abortion advocates, homosexuals, and their "godless" protectors and putative sponsors—liberals, humanists, civil libertarians, secularists, and that hotbed of Christian "apostasy" and one-world heresy, the National Council of Churches, which inexplicably includes most of America's major Protestant and Eastern Orthodox denominations, Southern Baptists excepted.

The election of Ronald Reagan and a chastened Congress puts the New Right within striking distance of its social agenda. While the President and his advisors might wish the whole issue would go away, as divisive and distracting from economic and military policy, politicians like Senators Jesse Helms and Paul Laxalt are too deeply committed, and too much in political debt to the "Library Court" and other religious rightists, to stop short of success.

Constitutional amendments to ban abortion and to mandate prayer in the public school are *minimum* objectives. Much more could follow, and much is likely to follow by legislative enactment. Thus the most powerful, best financed, and most elaborately organized drive for the piecemeal repeal of the Bill of Rights in American history is under way. If the right fails on one initiative, it is certain to return to the battle with a revision.

How successful this onslaught will be in abrogating the pluralism and freedom of American society is far from certain. The same fear of political reprisal by single-issue voting blocs that is eroding opposition in Congress is felt even more strongly by most state legislators. Once such amendments move out of the House and Senate to the legislatures of the various states, the state houses can fall like dominoes before the onslaught of the pro-prayer and anti-abortion lobbies. This effect is what the New Right strategy is designed to produce by delivering a "bullet vote" on the so-called moral issues. For American women in their child-bearing years the threat to freedom of choice in having children is immediate, massive, and devastating.

Once the strategy proves to work on such prominent issues as prayer and outlawing abortion, the levee will have been breached and the floods of antiliberal repeal can wash over any other article of the Constitution that stands in the way of rightist religious ascendancy. If "public decency" and "Christian faith" are offended by untoward freedom of the press, an appropriate amendment can be brought forth to restrict publications that run counter to popular sensibilities. One must not assume that only sexually oriented material would be affected.

The lack of a serious "antipornography" amendment restricting press freedom is surprising, except that to press forward on that front at present would take too much wind out of the sails to bring religious devotions into the public schools and to prohibit abortion, both measures alleged to be necessary because of the "moral decline" fostered by humanistic secularism and liberal tolerance.

That this scenario is not exaggerated can be sustained by considering the view of one of the nation's foremost constitutional authorities, Leo Pfeffer, special counsel of the American Jewish Congress. In a 1981 interview with Betty Brout, editor of the *Bulletin* of the Moral Democracy movement (a coalition to counter right-wing religious intolerance), Dr. Pfeffer expressed alarm at the drive to amend the Constitution, viewing the chances for passage as most serious.

> Many of the New Right or Moral Majority have made anti-abortion a one-issue test of acceptability for election or re-election to political office; and given their financial resources, it is certainly possible that they will be able to muster support from the voters for their position. From here on, it is not a matter

of pursuing any possible legal remedy; there aren't any. Rather, it is now a political issue, with a need to bring pressure to bear where it will help.

We must work to defeat this amendment in the Congress. . . . It is much harder to lobby in every state than in the Congress. Should this amendment get to the states, given the money and organizational skill of the New Right, they may very well succeed in getting 38 states to ratify.

For the benefit of those who are unaware that a decisive constitutional amendment would block further judicial intervention by the courts, Pfeffer emphasizes that the currently proposed amendment would clearly empower the states to restrict or abolish abortion by whatever legislative enactment they may please. "Abortion would be effectively outlawed in the United States. Some states might have more rigid laws than others, but in the main abortion would be illegal." Pfeffer sees passage of such an amendment accelerating the drive for a laundry list of New Right constitutional abridgments. School prayer, anti-evolution—or at least the weakening of scientific teaching by forcing equal time for pseudo-scientific "creationism"—tax support for non-public education, and prohibition of school busing to achieve desegregation are among the measures he enumerates.

Conceivably the new Right might bring pressure to bear to repeal or nullify the Fifth Amendment ban on self-incrimination. There is already vocal opposition to this protection, and it is not impossible to believe that an American citizen may be compelled to testify against himself or herself. Any drive to abridge rights and freedoms in one area gives rise to similar efforts in other areas. All of which makes this proposed amendment even more dangerous than it seems on the surface.

The grim prospect that Pfeffer foresees following passage of an antiabortion amendment may seem unlikely to Americans with a more optimistic view of the political system's historic capacity to correct its course when extremes prevail. But there is no assurance that the tides of McCarthyism, which have risen dangerously high before, must necessarily recede before doing irreparable harm to the Constitution's protection of individual rights or social and religious pluralism. Given the demonstrated power of mobilized pressure groups to swing elections and dictate terms to a less involved majority, there is no necessary security in public opinion polls that consistently show virtually a two-to-one majority favoring a woman's right to choose an abortion.

The appropriate and necessary response to the "Library Court" mobilization of "pro-family" antiabortion forces on which Viguerie and Weyrich pin their hopes is a two-part program of public education and counteraction. The educational aspect is primary and requires the tedious and tireless work of debunking right-wing whispering campaigns, slanders, and distortions. It is not necessary or appropriate to match their use of character assassination or misleading characterization.

Intolerance cannot be tolerated in a decent society, but it must be combated by principled and ethical means. As William Gilbert understood, "Let the punishment fit the crime." For the extreme right, exposing their own words to wide public scrutiny is punishment enough.

When Senator Helms declares, "Your tax dollars are being used to pay grade school classes that teach our children that cannibalism, wife-swapping and the murder of infants and the elderly are acceptable behavior," the most gullible may believe him and swell with indignation at "Satanic" humanist and liberal educators. But a better informed and more thoughtful audience immediately recognizes that the senator is "pulling a fast one." The most severe punishment for such blunderbuss tactics is to give public attention to statements aimed at a special audience deemed safe for manipulation. Political confidence men, like moray eels, like to slash at their victims from the protected cover of a concealing reef.

Because sex arouses the strongest moral feelings, it is on issues related to sex that the extreme right seeks to galvanize popular indignation and hysteria. The answer to this induced frenzy is to state the facts as clearly and fairly as possible.

When popular television evangelists such as James Robison and Jerry Falwell try to portray sex education, abortion rights, and a more rational attitude toward divorce, homosexuality, and premarital sex as inventions of "godless" secularists secretly plotting national decay, they must be answered by the countervailing consciences and intellects of respected Catholic, Protestant, and Jewish religious leaders or lay people. The American Humanist Association cannot answer the slander, no matter how worthy and innocent individual humanists may be.

The Religious Coalition for Abortion Rights and other groups accept this responsibility. They recognize they must "talk sense" in moral and religious terms to their own people in the churches and synagogues. (A number of organizations working toward this end are identified in the Afterword.)

Among the uncelebrated heroines of the abortion rights cause are the women of Catholics for a Free Choice. A majority of all Catholics support freedom of choice, and among younger Catholics of the child-bearing years the percentage is substantially higher.

Lisa Desposito, co-founder and frequent spokeswoman of the New York State branch of this Catholic lay organization states flatly:

> Certainly the Catholic bishops have the right, indeed the obligation, to address moral issues—just as all religious leaders do. But given the lack of religious, scientific, legal, and medical consensus with regard to abortion and the point at which a fetus becomes a person, no single view should be written into law. To do so negates the meaning of a pluralistic society.

Reflecting on the history of uncertainty within the church about the moment when personhood comes into being, Desposito observes:

The Catholic church itself has not always agreed on what has now become an immovable position on the part of the hierarchy. While human life has always been sacred, how many informed Catholics know that, for most of church history, there has been divided opinion on the exact moment of ensoulment of the fetus, hence personhood? Traditional church position, based on Aquinas, supported the theory of delayed ensoulment, holding that it occurs later in the course of fetal development. The church has always opposed abortion, not because the fetus is a person, but as part of a code of sexual ethics which views abortion as a sin of sex.

Lisa Desposito might have added, for those unfamiliar with traditional Christian doctrine, that all sexual activity that did not have procreation as its object was regarded as sin. On this basis the church still opposes artificial birth control, although curiously the "natural" rhythm method has been approved. Catholic youths were instructed, as are fundamentalist Protestant young people, that onanism (masturbation or premature withdrawal) is a sin that God punished with death in the case of the unfortunate Onan, whose fate is told in the book of Genesis.

Ms. Desposito sharply challenges the claim of the Bishops to speak for the laity:

Contrary to popular belief that there is unanimity among Catholics in opposition to legal abortion, every poll has indicated a divided church, with the hierarchy and the laity holding opposite beliefs. . . . Seventy seven per cent of American Catholics believe that the decision is a personal one between a woman and her doctor, that it is not the business of the government.

In her judgment, "The Roman Catholic hierarchy is actively participating in the politicizing of the abortion issue. It is also a time during which the New Right has seized upon the complexities of the abortion issue and is using them to further their own—and separate—political agenda." She notes that in the spring of 1981, Italy, a nation that is 95 percent Catholic, voted "overwhelmingly" to affirm the right to legal abortion.

Lisa Desposito does not underestimate the struggle and pain of the Catholic faithful who dissent from the leaders of their church. She admits that her decision to support freedom of conscience on abortion and contraception "did not happen overnight; as with most Catholics, it evolved over a period of years. Even then, I remained silent within the church family and in public."

For this courageous Catholic woman, the issue is exactly what it is for women of every faith or belief who make the decision to stand up for abortion rights:

> For pro-choice Catholics the answer is the primacy of conscience. We believe that the First Amendment of the Constitution, which guarantees religious liberty, provides a legal right to abortion as an option. . . . We believe that each and every woman, with the guidance of the important others in her life, must be free to decide for herself and must have access to a legal means to carry out that decision.

Desposito's concern for the "important others" belies the religious right's contention that women seeking abortion rights are hedonists and nihilists with no moral principle other than pleasing themselves. On the contrary, she cites approvingly a pro-choice priest who during the Italian referendum stated: "There are many ways of living religion. . . . Abortions are sometimes done for love . . . women have love for their families, for society and for other children."

The religious spirit has never been confined to professional custodians of the established cult. Consider the great prophets of ancient Israel, often lay figures with no official standing or authority, who challenged the righteousness of the temple priesthood in the name of a higher law of justice and mercy.

Were they the "secular humanists" and "agents of Satan" of their generations? Certainly the biblical prophets were forced into exile and frequently murdered at the instigation of the establishment of altar and throne.

Similarly, in ancient Athens, Socrates was condemned for "atheism" and centuries later early Christians were denounced in Rome on the same charge. Whoever diverged from custom and authority was an atheist and a "hater of the human race." For being an "enemy of the people" in Stalinist Russia, millions of hapless political dissenters and innocent suspects were executed or languished in Siberian prisons.

The theocratic law of the doctrinaire right and the "proletarian" law of the dictatorial left spring from the same poisonous source of social pathology and have identical effect: To deprive human beings of personal choice and rational self-direction in the name of a superior law entrusted to a spiritual or ideological elite. Throughout history, ancient and modern, it has been an unfailing formula for moral sterility, oppression, and death.

6

UNFIT FOR CHILDREN:
Controlling the Classroom

Schoolchildren in America are being taught that it is right to lie, cheat, steal, and kill. They are being brainwashed by their teachers to believe that anything is right if you like it. There are no objective moral principles. So if you want to do something because it feels good, do it. Anything goes. This is the basic philosophy of values clarification, sex education, drug abuse education, and public school teaching generally under the aegis of the liberal, humanistic educators who have captured control. American parents must fight back, or else face reality and remove their children to private schools under conservative religious direction.

Is this the true state of affairs in the American public school? Yes, if we are to believe the chorus of voices from the right, ranging from the Moral Majority and other religious New Right organizations to such old right perennials as the John Birch Society. Indeed, most of the arguments and many of the horror stories about "humanistic" education now being circulated by New Right religious and educational lobbies and pressure groups have simply been recycled from publications of the Birch Society and other far-right organizations.

The number and influence of such right-wing "educational" lobbies and action groups have multiplied in recent years.

Teachers and friends of public education are alarmed that the goals of classroom censorship and right-wing control of local school boards may be realized unless an informed public understands the issues and moves to support academic freedom in the classroom. What are the objectives of the educational right-wing? Among them, censorship of library books (not just to remove obscene material but to monitor social and intellectual philosophies as well), the abolition of sex education, forcing the teaching of the fundamentalist doctrine of creation disguised as "creation science," and eliminating the teaching of ethics or values by the method of stimulating the child's powers of moral reasoning.

If the above seems overdrawn, consider this widely quoted portrayal of public education circulated by an organization called the Network of Patriotic Letter Writers of Pasadena, California:

> IT'S OK TO LIE—IT'S OK TO STEAL—IT'S OK TO HAVE
> PREMARITAL SEX—IT'S OK TO CHEAT—IT'S OK TO KILL
> —if these things are a part of *your own* values system and you
> have clarified these values to yourself. The important thing is not
> *what* values to choose, but that you have *chosen them* yourself.
> . . . That in essence is what values clarifiers teach children in
> schools today.

Right-wing opponents of values clarification publicly burned forty copies of a book setting forth its principles and methods. While book burning may be an isolated phenomenon in America, the crusade against what has come to be known as humanistic education is a major concern to educators and defenders of academic freedom. Teachers unions and professional educational organizations are being forced to defend both their methods of teaching and their personal integrity and loyalty to the nation.

Always just below the surface and often rising above it is the accusation that humanistic educators are inspired by totalitarian philosophies and harbor subversive intentions. In an article entitled, "Why Johnny Can't Tell Right From Wrong" in the November, 1981, issue of *Conquest*, published by the Kansas City Youth for Christ, Margaret Baldwin writes:

> Although it has many names and disguises such as values education, moral education, citizenship education, moral development, and character education, values clarification is the hedonistic grandchild of Communist brainwashing and the offspring of sensitivity training. Using this powerful psychological technique, humanists are seeking to replace the traditional values of the school children of the United States with situation ethics.

Baldwin further tells us: "A basic assumption which teachers and students are to accept is that no idea is wrong, no matter how immoral or ludicrous."

This innuendo that humanistic educators and philosophers have no moral standards, are Communists, Communist dupes, and/or enemies of the American heritage who have set out to undermine the character of the nation's youth, is a basic feature of the radical right's prosecution of its case against modern methods or humanistic values in education.

Sometimes the indictment becomes too fatuous to require refutation. Thus, to enable their followers to spot curricula designed by humanists, the National Congress for Educational Excellence listed some three hundred words or concepts they suggest will help unmask the dreaded humanistic infection in education. In his book *Censors in the Classroom* (Southern Illinois University Press), Edward B. Jenkinson selects fifty of these "give-away" terms to show the absurdity of the case. Humanists, we are told, are people whose vocabularies will give prominence to such terms as academic freedom, accountability, analysis, behavior, body language, conflict, citizenship, creative writing, democracy, discovery method, emotions, and so forth. Human growth, problem-solving, self-understanding, and values are among the terms that can help expose an educator as a humanist. Are we reaching a state of affairs in which teachers will speak of democracy, citizenship, accountability or problem-solving at the risk of their jobs?

Not only are particular words and concepts to be regarded with suspicion by right-thinking citizens; entire academic disciplines are suspect. According to Jenkinson's study of inquisitors and their targets, anthropology, Black studies, ethnic studies, the humanities, individualized instruction, moral education, psychology, and sociology are included with, of course, those familiar bogeymen, sex education and values clarification. Why so much attention to values clarification? What is it, and why is it so widely feared by those of the political and religious right?

Values clarification is the name of a technique or method of moral education based on John Dewey's principle that effective learning involves thinking about one's experience; it seeks to use the young person's powers of observation and reasoning to examine attitudes about behavioral questions. For example, is it right to lie or steal? Is it ever right, under any circumstances, to mislead or deceive, even to save an innocent human life? Would it ever be right, under any circumstances whatever, to steal a loaf of bread? Is it usually right to tell falsehoods or to take what does not belong to you? If not, why not? How do we decide that one act is right and another wrong?

These questions were not invented by the small group of teachers who only a few years ago developed the technique of teaching now known as values clarification. Their method of teaching by asking questions and examining the answers is as old as Socrates, their emphasis on the consequences for human beings as a standard of judgment at least as ancient as the New Testament teaching that the Sabbath was made for man, not man for the Sabbath.

When values clarification was first attacked, it appears from their literature that proponents believed they were simply the victims of mistaken identity: they were being confused with the atheistic or agnostic advocates of the religion or life philosophy known as "secular humanism." In their defense they quickly pointed out that they were not humanists in that meaning of the word. Thousands of their teachers and thinkers were priests, ministers, and rabbis, or lay members of traditional religions.

There is no question that the radical right endeavored to confuse the issue by throwing humanistic religious groups, such as many Unitarian Universalists, Ethical Culturists, and other "nontheistic" humanists, into the same bag with groups having no religious connotation or connection.

But the opposite was also true: Ethical Culturists and humanists who may have had their own reservations about the adequacy or sufficiency of values clarification for moral education, just as unexpectedly found themselves under assault as presumed advocates of the "moral relativism" and "situation ethics" which the values clarifiers were accused of teaching. (It should be pointed out that Ethical Culture, the oldest of the organizations in America officially affiliated with the "secular-religious" humanist movement, as represented in the International Humanist and Ethical Union, was founded by a Kantian ethical idealist, Felix Adler, who was uncompromising in his rejection of moral relativism.)

Thus, the extreme right attacks values clarification by attributing to its developers a religious position that most of them do not hold while also claiming that the values clarification movement, from which many religious and secular humanists emphatically dissent, represents the official ethical philosophy of humanism—which the religious right further narrows down to "situation ethics."

The truth of the matter is not so simple. Most religious and secular humanists, those accepting humanism as their religion or life philosophy, would recognize the usefulness of values clarification as an educational tool in awakening the powers of critical thinking essential for moral growth and for participation in democratic dialogue. These are the stalwart Jeffersonian traits of reasonable discussion and the untrammeled testing of ideas, without which a free classroom, or a free society, cannot exist. At the same time those who embrace humanism as a personal religion or life philosophy would go well beyond values clarification in asserting a distinctive moral philosophy they are prepared to defend on rational grounds. The principles of such an ethical faith include upholding the worth of each person as a unique moral agent in a community of unique selves, and the values of freedom, reason, and tolerance within a free society. From such an ethical system it follows that needlessly, wilfully inflicting avoidable pain, harm, or death on any creature is always evil; denying the moral freedom or dignity of human beings is universally wrong; serving to advance the development of free, self-directed, socially responsible human beings within a mutually supportive democratic community of such persons is the greatest good. Is this situation ethics? Perhaps, with sufficient qualification, it is, but not as the radical right misinterprets and abuses a moral philosophy that they appear to be incapable or unwilling to describe fairly.

Most decent human beings accept "situation ethics" if that means believing we would be right in not disclosing to the Gestapo the direction in which the fugitive Jew ran into the forest. We could, under those circumstances, deceive the would-be killer of the innocent and sleep with clear consciences; but if, on the contrary, we became the killer's collaborators by a misapplied rectitude, we could not sleep. If this is what situation ethics means—and in fact this is what its proponents have in mind when they use the term—then most human beings as a matter of course practice situation ethics and are completely justified in doing so. But this does not mean that we lie, steal, or kill in any but the most morally tortured and extreme circumstances, and only then to avoid committing a greater wrong.

To point this out, and to enable students to grasp the moral dilemmas that arise when two or more moral principles are in conflict, is not to concede that humanistic moral philosophers have no principles, or that their highest value is mere sensual pleasure or self-expression. Morally autonomous persons, the goal of humanistic ethics, means people capable of self-determination, responsible self-governance; it does not mean just "doing your own thing," as uninformed or deliberately misleading critics claim. But such misrepresentations fly with the wind because of their usefulness to extremist propagandists.

Howard Kirschenbaum, who with Sidney Simon and a small group of other educators achieved national recognition for developing the values clarification curriculum, observes that many teachers, administrators, and school boards are "totally baffled" when accused of teaching "the religion of secular humanism." In recent years, he reveals, he has received many letters and calls asking for help from teachers and school officials under attack.

> They may not know what secular humanism is. If they do, they probably don't consider themselves secular humanists. They can't understand how anyone could make such a charge against their school district.
>
> They don't know what is behind such an attack or criticism, or who or how many people are involved, or how best to handle it. They probably don't realize that what they are experiencing is part of a well-organized, national campaign and that educators in hundreds of districts across the country are in precisely the same situation.

Dr. Kirschenbaum summarizes some of the points he makes in meeting such attack:

> I begin by acknowledging that there is such a thing as secular humanism. The Supreme Court has suggested as much. I explain

that secular humanism is *not* the same thing as "humanistic education," although the two terms are often confused because of a common Latin root, *humanus*, meaning human.

Secular humanism is a religion or life philosophy; humanistic education refers to various educational approaches often used in the schools. I point out that most educators consider themselves in the Judeo-Christian religious tradition and that relatively few educators regard themselves as secular humanists; although the latter have a right to their religious views too.

As one of the principals of the values clarification curriculum, Kirschenbaum, like his collaborators, is often depicted as an evil genius bent on corrupting American youth.

In situations where my own religious or moral integrity is being impugned, either directly or through innuendo, I frequently point out that I believe in God, that my religious and moral code is very important to me, and that I resent the type of dogmatic position which automatically attacks the integrity and character of those with whom it differs.

I point out that, although the attack on secular humanism is at least ten years old, with many legal battles, the courts have never found that secular humanism was being taught in the public schools.

In order to meet the assault not only upon values clarification but upon other aspects of academic freedom, Kirschenbaum and others have organized the National Coalition for Democracy in Education, headquartered in Saratoga Springs, New York. Kirschenbaum serves as the organization's executive director.

Writing nearly twenty years ago in their book, *The Strange Tactics of Extremism* (W. W. Norton and Co., New York), Harry and Bonaro Overstreet warned readers and those subject to attack to be alert to slippery writing, slurs, and broad assertions with no factual reference. Radical right propaganda today lives upon "slippery writing, slurs and broad assertions," as its extremist forerunners have always done. Examples abound in books such as Homer Duncan's

Secular Humanism: The Most Dangerous Religion in America and *The Siecus Circle: A Humanist Revolution,* by Clair Chambers, published by Western Islands Press of Belmont, Massachusetts, a publisher of Birch Society literature. (Incidentally, this 506-page book, a veritable catalogue of alleged humanist mischief in support of sex education, abortion rights, and similar issues, identifies the present writer as a "prominent Humanist" and includes a lengthy quotation from a 1969 article that I wrote for the *Humanist* magazine on Supreme Court rulings affecting the rights of conscience of nontheistic humanists. The same book treats many liberal educators and humanist philosophers as un-American, participants in "a round of subversion," "Communist fronters," etc.)

Tricky language and fuzzy logic to make clearly different or even opposite philosophies appear to be the same becomes a fine art in far-right political theologizing. At times the whirlpool of ideas becomes dizzying.

Thus, Mary Royer, in *Public Education: River of Pollution* introduces some eddies and rapids that would be difficult for even a crew of philosophical Argonauts to navigate with a clear head:

> We . . . conclude with one singular inescapable fact: dialectical materialism, and Darwinism, have exceedingly strong roots in both Hedonism and Humanism, for both Hedonism and Humanism have flowered and taken on vigorous life under the later thesis and antithesis of dialectical materialism. Each is firmly and unmistakably interconnected, for the latter evolved from the former, and it is the whole of the philosophies of Hedonism, Humanism, Darwinism and dialectical materialism which run rife throughout large segments of that system of progressive education, which includes various social studies courses, as well as studies in the humanities.

Such concatenations pass for philosophical analysis among the gurus of the far right. In a single breathless sentence she descends the rapids of the "river of pollution" and in a *tour de force* connects into a single stream dialectical materialism (the official philosophy of Marxism-Leninism), Darwinism, Hedonism, Humanism, progressive education, and "various social studies courses, as well as studies in the humanities." That list of subjects dangerous to your ideological health leaves a very basic curriculum of limited reading, safe writing, and plain arithmetic, taking care that the reading and writing do not stray into the region of the forbidden "isms" or the perilous social studies and humanities.

While humanistic education is treated as a product of Communist ideology, it is traced by most right-wing critics to the educational theories of John Dewey, whose philosophy of democratic pragmatism was deeply rooted in the American experience of pluralism and respect for individual differences. But as we encounter so many times in rightist thinking, contradiction and self-cancelling arguments pose no obstacles.

In Montgomery County, Maryland, the mania to search out and destroy the illusive "religion of secular humanism" in public education, prompted the State Board of Education to undertake a twenty-one month investigation at a cost of $200,000. Over 1600 pages of documentation concluded with a finding of no evidence that secular humanism was being taught in the public school.

The Director of the Baptist Joint Committee on Public Affairs, representing most of the Baptist bodies in the United States, declared that the teaching of secular humanism in public education is a myth. Responsible representatives of other major religious bodies have reached the same conclusion, dismissing the whole affair as a concoction of the radical right designed to attack ideas in public education that run counter to their social doctrines. Thus, the American Heritage Foundation, a right-wing "educational foundation" funded substantially by Joseph Coors, who with his wife donated the institution's headquarters building in Washington, D.C., continues to press the discredited charge: "The public is growing more aware of the inequity of using tax dollars for the support of nontheistic religion. Secular humanism in the schools is indeed an issue whose time has come." In the making of propaganda, bare-faced assertion serves as effectively as fact.

After a long dormancy, organized opposition to the objective study of biological evolution dogs the teaching of science. The common argument runs that evolution is a "doctrine" of humanist and materialist philosophy wholly lacking a scientific foundation. Darwin, identified as a humanist and nonbeliever, is portrayed as the inventor of a hoax or delusion, which through the work of secular educators is being employed to destroy the nation by means of destroying its religion.

The statements of eminent scientists are removed from context to make it appear that their acceptance of evolution is weak or based on extra-scientific considerations. Thus, Darwin's most celebrated champion, Thomas Henry Huxley, is cited as holding that "evolution was not an established theory but a tentative hypothesis, an extremely valuable and even probable hypothesis, but a hypothesis none the less." The unsuspecting reader would not know that Huxley's observation came early in the history of evolutionary investigation and that more than a century of research has strengthened a thousandfold the case for evolution, drawing from many biological and geological sciences that did not even exist in the time of Darwin and Huxley.

Antievolutionists frequently make their case seem plausible by abusing the word "theory" as it is used in science. In their usage a theory is only an unsubstantiated speculation, instead of the coherent body of tested and confirmed knowledge that has standing as a theory in science.

Because the method of science also requires that conflicting hypotheses about the specific mechanisms and processes of evolution be openly debated in scientific journals, each disagreement or revision of theory is taken as evidence that evolutionary biologists do not know what they are talking about. Fundamentalist "creationists," on the other hand, have no such doubts: The universe and life, including human life, were created in the manner specified in the biblical account of *Genesis*, read as a literal record. The human species, like all others before it, was thus the result of miraculous creation. There is no line of descent from other species. Each species represents an act of creation *de novo*, and it was all accomplished only a few thousand years before Christ.

Unlike the antievolutionists of a half-century ago, present-day creationists are not attempting to forbid the teaching of evolution, although it is an ominous sign of their power to intimidate school boards and textbook publishers that a major publisher, Harcourt Brace Jovanovich, is reported to have eliminated all mention of Charles Darwin in three of its recent texts, a feat comparable to recounting the discovery of America without Columbus. Another publisher reduced by a third the treatment of evolution in a 1977 text it issued.

Since outlawing the teaching of evolution is no longer feasible, antievolutionists have concentrated on gaining a "balanced treatment" for their fundamentalist doctrine of creation. To enable the doctrine, if possible, to withstand judicial challenge, the biblical belief has been renamed "creation science," with the pretension that it is a nonreligious "scientific" concept, although there is no big secret about where creationists find the outline of their "theory." Both scientists and theologians have rejected this disguise, and a Federal judge in Arkansas concurred. In the Arkansas case, a law requiring the teaching of "creation science" was immediately challenged after passage in 1981 by a broad group of Catholic, Protestant, and Jewish theologians who contended that creation science is not a science but a particular form of religious belief being taught in violation of the First Amendment and denying nonfundamentalist religions equal treatment.

Supporting this argument, a professor of the philosophy of science, Michael E. Ruse, testified that creation science is clearly a religion, not a science, since it is based on supernaturalist beliefs and is not subject to scientific testing for validity. Professor Ruse noted that "it invokes miracles" as an explanation of natural phenomena and thus must be classified as a religion rather than a science. "Nobody is saying religion is false," he contended. "They are saying it is not a science."

By the end of 1981 similar bills to require the teaching of creation science had been introduced into at least eighteen of the fifty state legislatures. Despite their setback in the Arkansas Federal courtroom, creationists continue their effort.

It should be remembered that the basic objection of philosophers of science and civil libertarians to such laws is not directed to the particular merit, or lack of merit, of creationism. Whether that concept is good or bad science is not open to political solution. Civilization should be finished with the medieval practice of having councils of bishops or parliaments ruling whether the earth is flat, the stars fixed, witches supernaturally propelled through the air, or illness caused by demons. Creationists are free to make their case in the give-and-take of scientific research and deliberation. If their views are valid, their doctrine will survive on its merit. If not, no law can give it credence except among authoritarians who confuse political coersion with truth.

From Copernicus and Galileo to a generation of Soviet geneticists persecuted by Stalin, we can see the dismal record of "science" by political command. The Nazis could not abide the "Jewish" science of Einstein. It is not the business of government to have clerks policing the thoughts of Darwins and Einsteins.

Noting the range and the power of the fundamentalist assault on the public school, Betty Brout, writing in the *Moral Democracy Bulletin*, commented: "The attack on public education by the New Right seems to be taking on the characteristics of an octopus." Counting off some of the principal points in the New Right campaign, she noted:

> The issues now include the massive drive to legislate prayer in the public classroom; the push to enact laws allowing tax tuition credits for the support of non-public schools; the bitter controversy over the teaching of "creationism" as science on a par with evolution; the steam gathering to ban busing—with no accompanying safeguards to insure unsegregated public education; and the censorship of textbooks and school libraries to keep books that children read pure from the viewpoint of the Religious Right.

With a touch of humor she noted that the book censors sometimes reveal their complete ignorance of the contents of the books they propose to ban, pointing to a *New York Times* story reporting a right-winger's index of forbidden books that include two suggestive titles: *Mr. and Mrs. Pig's Evening Out*, an innocent children's story of porcine domesticity, and *Making It with Mademoiselle*, which proved to be a home-sewing instruction book for teenagers published by *Mademoiselle* magazine.

Howard Kirschenbaum offers counsel to bring reason to the controversy. He echoes the advice of the Overstreets not to answer extremists by imitating their methods, or by becoming shrill in defending one's own position or integrity when under attack. And finally, he comments, "If people have criticisms about courses or textbooks, there are proper channels for exploring their grievances. Creating a phony issue such as secular humanism, however, will help no one and will only divert valuable energies away from education."

Wise as such advise may be, we cannot expect the true believers of the militant right to accept it. To engage in reasonable dialogue, accepting their opponents' good faith and decency, would require them to abandon their drive to overturn the pluralistic secular character of American public education. They show little sign of such a change of heart.

7

THE GREAT ARMS RACE:
The Holy War Against Communism

In recent years the belief has been promoted that the United States is dangerously behind the Soviet Union in nuclear arms—so far behind, it is argued, that this country is becoming a tempting target. This view has been advanced especially by the political right, although it is not confined to those on the right. Nevertheless, the New Right has added its ideological burden in the demand to achieve military dominance in order to "roll back Communism" in Central Europe, raising again the specter in Soviet minds that aggressive groups in the United States still harbor the goal of using armed intervention or the threat of intervention, backed by nuclear weapons, to enforce a political ultimatum.

At the same time that the right seeks to return the world to a posture of Cold War in Europe, it undermines our recently established good relations with the People's Republic of China through continuing attachment to the idea of alliance with a militant Nationalist China on Taiwan. The pressure to supply the Nationalists with advanced aircraft threatens our accord with China and opens the prospect of once more facing unfriendly powers on two fronts.

To have the means to pursue this global policy of confrontation, it is argued by rightist strategists, the United States must regain its previous advantage in armaments. Richard Viguerie maintains: "Clearly we have fallen from being the Number One military power in the world to the Number Two power—behind a country whose leaders are totally committed to defeating America and conquering the world."

Despite a contrary opinion on the part of the uniformed defense chiefs, Viguerie is not only convinced that the Soviet Union has dangerously outstripped the United States in military power, but like many other spokesmen on the right, he is confident that liberals have willfully brought this about:

"Liberal presidents and liberal congresses have deliberately put us in second place, believing that America's overwhelming strength was a threat to the Soviets and world peace." In a deliberate design to "appease" the Russians, Viguerie argues, liberals "disarmed" America. Liberals, he concludes, "in effect, have issued an open invitation to increased Soviet aggression around the world."

Before the presidential and congressional elections of 1980, the New Right movement made massive rearmament a principal campaign issue. Viguerie expressed the commonly held right-wing position that detente must be abandoned: "In place of detente we need a policy of military superiority . . . combined with a multi-billion dollar effort to fight the Communists with propaganda in every country in the world."

"I believe," he wrote, "we must return to a World War II emergency of rebuilding our military position. . . . It would mean a total commitment by everyone from the President to the worker on the job and a realization that we are at war with a dangerous enemy."

To be certain we grasp the point of the enormous buildup required, Viguerie confides that we are "locked in world-wide combat with Communism. In fact, . . . we have been fighting the Third World War since before the Second World War ended." He urges such overwhelming military power that the

Western powers can "demand" free elections and Soviet withdrawal from Eastern Europe. Viguerie credits Anthony Dolan, who served as special assistant to Ronald Reagan's campaign director, William Casey (now CIA Director), with setting out the terms of such "initiatives" in an article in the May, 1980, issue of *National Review*. While disclaiming the intention to resort to military threats or action to compel this disgorgement, the Dolan plan as recommended by Viguerie would, among other steps, have the United States Ambassador to the United Assembly make a demand for the removal of Soviet forces from Eastern Europe as well as Afghanistan. To support this demand the President would "announce a new form of 'linkage,'" tying future negotiations with the Soviet Union to withdrawal from Eastern Europe. Anti-Communist propaganda would be greatly increased through such channels as Radio Free Europe and Radio Liberty.

Viguerie cites the argument of Christian anti-Communist crusader, Dr. Fred Schwarz, that an expenditure of $1.4 billion for a propaganda offensive, equal to one percent of the United States military budget before the Reagan increases, would work "miracles" in deflating Communism. The psychological, diplomatic, and military consequences of raising the recrimination and bombast of the Cold War to such a high pitch are hardly considered by New Right intellectuals and publicists such as Dolan, Viguerie, and Schwarz.

"Free America from arms control restraints," urges Viguerie, "which perpetuate U.S. military inferiority and force us to fight the Third World War by Soviet rules." He is clear that we are fully involved in such a war and that we must pursue it to win. Accommodation and co-existence are out, because of the nature and aims of Communism.

New Right "think tanks" that develop schemes for pursuing the Third World War on terms they imagine can be aggressively managed, yet always controlled short of all-out military conflict, attribute to the Soviets a remarkable gift for composure and self-control. As we heat up the diplomatic and propaganda fronts against them, all the while pursuing the arms buildup with a commitment reminiscent of World War II, the Soviets are expected to come to their senses and accept the inevitability of our triumph, or else be run into the ground through sheer exhaustion.

The recklessness and sheer hubris of this ideologue's vision of things to come leaves totally out of reckoning the anxiety and restiveness that pursuit of such a policy would generate in the rest of the world, especially among our closest allies and now friendly neutrals. In fact, this early fruit of New Right bellicosity has already begun to ripen. Candidate Reagan's apparent adoption of the diplomatic and military stance of the New Right caused such an upheaval of neutralist and antinuclear feeling among the populations of America's Western allies that before the President had been in the office a year, the Soviets were clearly winning the battle for the mind in Western Europe. The President was forced to change his public posture and come to the negotiating table with his own proposal for nuclear arms reduction in Europe. This initiative was strongly urged by those in the State Department and White House who saw the political devastation in Europe produced by the Administration's truculence.

Two parties emerged among the President's advisors, one of which, reportedly headed by Secretary of State Alexander Haig, argued that a pragmatic approach was necessary, in contrast to the uncompromising hard line of the New Right true believers. Many moderate-to-liberal observers, as well as some conservatives, were surprised to see the Secretary of State, long a media symbol of hawkishness and martinet rigidity, suddenly emerge as the voice of reasonableness. It should have been remembered, however, that General Haig, after his unhappy role in the last weeks of the Nixon White House, had served effectively as the commander of NATO. He came to the Cabinet with greater knowledge and experience in dealing with European problems and perceptions than other presidential advisors, and he was not a member of the ultraconservative bloc that had pushed forward Ronald Reagan's political career.

Even without the differences of philosophy and rivalries within the President's political family, the realities of official responsibility and the conflicting claims and demands of allied countries and neutrals were bound to force the President to modify his approach in dealing with the Soviet bloc.

Campaign speeches and folksy images of standing up for our rights and competing to win do not add up to a policy. Thus, the struggle for the mind of Ronald Reagan had to begin. It came into the open in the President's first major foreign policy speech in November, 1981, in which he put forward the Administration's proposal for reduction of nuclear forces staged in Europe.

The thesis that candidate Reagan had accepted as his own, of a continuing, irrepressible struggle to be waged relentlessly between Communism and anti-Communism, is not a new article of faith in the rightist theology. It was already a fixed conviction during the Cold War thirty years ago. Combined with the claim of many New Right spokesmen that liberal leaders have been guilty of deliberately weakening America —and of consciously forbidding American forces to win in Vietnam, as allegedly in Korea twenty years earlier—the determination of the New Right to revive the Cold War becomes explicit.

But how sound is this approach, both in military terms and in relation to the political and economic contest between the West and the Soviet bloc? We might have hoped, and expected, that a generation of dealing with Communist nations would have enabled Americans to take a more balanced view of the Soviets and the limits of their power. But the doctrinaire right persists in viewing the Soviets as either on the verge of total collapse or standing ten feet tall.

Where military perceptions are involved, the Russians are always depicted as giants towering above a shrunken Western Europe defenseless except for a skimpy American shield. When in his first major foreign policy speech President Reagan offered to withdraw plans to station medium-range nuclear weapons in Western Europe if the Soviets would dismantle theirs, by his selection of data he reinforced the image of Soviet power as overwhelming.

At the President's side was a graph to illustrate the comparative strength of American and Soviet nuclear arms. The bar on the graph depicting American strength was a stubby rectangle. The adjoining bar, representing Soviet nuclear might, loomed above it like a Manhattan high-rise towering above a block of town houses.

But what does such graphic artistry prove? That America is dangerously outclassed as a military power, thanks to "liberal" sell-out and appeasement, answer the partisans of the radical right. Others, who have looked more critically at American and foreign studies comparing U.S. and Soviet nuclear arms, take a more cautious view.

The reality of the situation is far more complicated than the President's six-to-one ratio would lead us to suppose. Most experts give a vastly different picture. Retired Ambassador George F. Kennan, for example, sees the bars representing U.S. and Soviet nuclear capability as fairly leaping off the top of the chart. Kennan calls the nuclear capacity of both nations "redundant" in power to destroy any potential adversary many times over.

In contrast to the picture the President painted of devastating United States military inferiority, General David C. Jones, Chairman of the Joint Chiefs of Staff, has stated that he would not exchange the American military position for that of the Soviet Union.

A United Nations study, completed in July, 1980, concluded that Soviet and American nuclear arsenals are so vast that either nation could be deprived of a major portion of its missiles as victim of a surprise attack and still possess the capacity to obliterate the attacker. The U.N. study, which drew its information and analysis from many sources, concluded that the management of nuclear war remains, and is likely to remain, unpredictable and uncontrollable:

> There exists today at least 40,000 to 50,000 nuclear weapons, the explosive power of which is believed to be equivalent to that of more than one million Hiroshima bombs or . . . some 13 billion tons of TNT, which represents more than 3 tons for every man, woman and child on earth. In spite of this, the number of warheads continues to increase. . . .

The United States arsenal is estimated to be 30,000 warheads of the 50,000 world total. Neither major power, the United Nations findings held, could unleash even a few nuclear weapons for limited tactical purposes without the danger of triggering a conflagration in which both combatants and much of the neighboring world would be consumed.

In the face of this state of affairs, carefully constructed graphs and charts that offer precise comparisons of nuclear strength become exercises in special pleading and ultimately of self-deception.

Put simply, the variables are so many, the array of weapons so diverse, and the escalation of conflict so unmanageable, that precise calibration of equivalent destructive power becomes impossible. Given the unknowns, any ingenious theorist can make a strong case for almost any position he favors. There is no reason to doubt that President Reagan's chart accurately depicted what it was designed to compare— a small segment of the nuclear spectrum that he wished to highlight—but it failed to convey a picture of the overall array of nuclear forces.

Nevertheless, President Reagan's speech was viewed as an important step in moving toward discussion on the reduction of nuclear weapons. It won the immediate praise of not only

Mr. Reagan's expected allies, such as Prime Minister Thatcher and Chancellor Schmidt, but of European critics who advocate the total abolition of nuclear weapons. Michael Foote, head of Britain's Labor Party and a veteran of the ban-the-bomb-movement, lauded the President's initiative, which he saw as increasing the prospects for successful arms reduction talks.

The President's first major speech on foreign policy was viewed as significant in indicating that he was willing to turn away from the militant, uncompromising stance of his campaign rhetoric, and that he sought to distance himself somewhat from the hard-liners of the ideological right who continue to pursue the aim of military confrontation and "rollback" of the Soviets.

But if one recognizes that the reality of the power balance in Europe is far more complex than the President depicted, his opening position becomes far less bold and forthcoming than at first appearance.

No one with any detailed knowledge of the balancing forces seriously believes that the Soviet advantage in nuclear power in Europe is six to one. The President arrived at this convenient disparity by what he chose to include in Soviet weaponry and by what he chose to ignore in the NATO arsenal.

It is hard to argue against equal forces, when maintaining a balance of forces is the objective. But, given the diversity of the many weapons involved, agreement on equal forces has proved over many years of argument to be beyond satisfactory definition. Furthermore, given the redundancy of the nuclear arsenals—the capacity to destroy the enemy many times over—the quest for "equal" power has proved to be a diversion of energy. Preoccupation with this illusive and probably fictional equality only blocks agreement while the race for larger and more destructive systems accelerates uncontrollably.

A more realistic view of the problem might be gained by considering the United Nations study cited earlier. There we see ably argued the fallacy of the quest for perfect balance as well as the folly of rushing into escalation.

The U.N. study, commissioned by the General Assembly in December, 1978, requested the Secretary General, with the assistance of qualified experts, to undertake "a comprehensive study on nuclear weapons." The group was chaired by the Swedish Ambassador to the United Nations, Anders Thunborg, and consisted of representatives of eleven other countries.

Issued in July, 1980, during an American presidential campaign, the report stated: "As long as reliance continues to be placed upon the concept of the balance of nuclear deterrence as a method of maintaining peace, the prospect of the future will always remain dark, menacing and as uncertain as the fragile assumptions upon which they are based."

Striking at the notion that Soviet and American missile systems can be clearly compared, the study noted that "the Strategic Arms Limitations Talks between the two superpowers have come to be based on the premise of nuclear parity and within the framework of a continued reliance on a balance of mutual deterrence." Yet, the report observes: "The weapon systems of the two superpowers are in fact asymmetrical in that they are not exactly similar in terms of operation, power or effectiveness."

What effectiveness means in this field is not always open to demonstration. Much of the argument against the ratification of SALT II, for example, rested on the much larger size of Soviet nuclear rockets, their greater "throw weight" or capacity to lift heavier loads. While some viewed this Soviet development of mammoth rockets as the necessary consequence of the more primitive design and weight of Soviet bombs, others viewed it as a counter strategy to America's land-based Titan and Minuteman missile silos. To have any chance of taking out an underground launching site, given the imperfect accuracy of existing rockets, Soviet missiles must carry extremely large warheads.

Such gargantuan weapons are not effective against bombers in the air or highly maneuverable, hard-to-find submarines, which could effectively destroy the Soviet Union even if most or all United States land-based missiles were eliminated in a Soviet attack. In his book *National Defense*, James Fallows quotes defense writer Fred Kaplan as saying that retiring Minuteman missiles from our arsenal would render the huge Soviet rockets obsolete. Fallows further cites former Chairman of the Joint Chiefs of Staff General Maxwell Taylor as arguing that "the most effective way to attain a higher degree of invulnerability would be to remove from American soil the most inviting targets for a surprise attack, our land-based ICBMs."

General Taylor's argument needs much more attention than it has received. The leaders of the Mormon Church grasped the logic of his argument in mobilizing opposition to the placing of MX missiles in Utah and Nevada, despite the fact that the Mormon leadership is generally regarded as politically conservative.

Mormon opposition to the presence of this weapon system, which has led no one to accuse Mormons of appeasement or Soviet sympathy, should help us to understand why Western Europeans have become militant in resisting plans to place intermediate-range missiles in their highly populated countries. When it comes to nuclear weapons in relation to regional security, more means less.

Fallows, whose book has received widespread comment, argues that an excessively large military budget is producing a poorer, less certain defense, as impractical, unreliable systems and equipment are elaborated. Fallows believes that a cheaper, more flexible, and safer option lies in greater use of smaller, quieter submarines and conventional low-flying aircraft more likely to elude radar. He documents the effectiveness of such craft in extensive military exercises.

Since Fallows made this point it has received new support from other military observers. In fact, according to Drew Middleton, military writer for the *New York Times*, the effectiveness of the cruise missile so worries the Soviets as a flexible, easy-to-use weapon that its development may pose "one of the biggest obstacles to conclusive results" in limiting intermediate range missiles in Europe. It provides the United States with a comparatively inexpensive weapon already in production, with a range of more than 1500 miles, which can be carried by aircraft to within striking distance of its target, or fired from sea or land. The Reagan plan to build 4,000 of these weapons gives the U.S. an advantage that will affect the nuclear balance at least until the end of the decade, according to a Brookings study and other analyses cited by Middleton.

There is additional reason to believe that more means less as the United States moves to assume a greater role in the protection of Western Europe. The result of our overweening prominence is to make military wards of our NATO allies, removing their responsibility and necessity to look after their own defense by conventional arms. They are treated as Lilliputians under the knees of a Soviet giant. Yet the combined population of the Western Europe NATO nations exceeds that of the Soviet Union, and their economies are more highly developed.

If the European allies need more tanks and antitank guns to offset the Red Army, they have the material and human resources to build and operate those forces. We do not need to introduce more and deadlier American nuclear weapons, including the neutron bomb, to compensate for the alleged weakness of Western European armies. To move in this direction reduces stability and invites a choice between neutralism and acceptance of the strategy of certain suicide.

There is very little reason, all things considered, to justify the belief that the Soviets have achieved, or are about to achieve, the commanding nuclear superiority enabling them to attack the United States or our allies with reasonable assurance of winning a first-strike victory.

The notion that the Soviets are less vulnerable to attack than we are is groundless. The theory that Soviet leaders, who saw their country devastated and 20,000,000 of their people killed in World War II, are ready to risk national suicide in a mad venture for world conquest is a wild speculation—the paranoid delusion of a political right that has lost perspective and is making a religion of confrontation.

There is plenty to criticize about the closed society of the Soviet Union. Indeed, the Western nations have an obligation to insist that Eastern bloc nations live up to the human-rights stipulations of the Helsinki accords, and to use world public opinion and diplomatic intervention to the utmost on behalf of suppressed political dissidents. But steps to change the system under which they live can only be brought about by internal popular pressures and passive resistance, and must be left to the political idealism and courage of the Poles, Czechs, Hungarians, Lithuanians, Ukranians, and the Russians themselves.

Heating up the old Cold War, reviving McCarthyism at home and beating the drums for confrontation abroad is regressive. It can serve no legitimate national interest or goal. It can only make our world radically more dangerous.

It should be apparent to anyone who takes the trouble to become acquainted with the facts of nuclear warfare and the vast scale of our armaments, that we do not need a race for more of the same on both sides. If the purpose of our gaining military supremacy is to force the Soviets to surrender their hold on the nations of Eastern Europe, such an objective requires very critical scrutiny—and rejection. In a world freighted with nuclear explosives, forcing a Soviet "rollback" risks rolling down the curtain on civilization.

If by beginning the process of talking with the Soviets the President is moving to separate himself from the nuclear militancy of his allies on the far right, and from his former campaign rhetoric, we have grounds for hope. But Mr. Reagan will have to move much more decisively toward a realistic and flexible policy to break the spell of thinking— and of leading others to think—that a race for more and more expensive nuclear arms can make us secure. The logic of nuclear-arms development has forced both Soviet leaders and American Presidents of both parties to recognize that a nuclear duel is unwinnable and that diplomacy alone can preserve civilization.

8

MONEY, POWER, AND IDEOLOGY:
Who's Left When America
Turns Right?

Senator Jesse Helms had reason to be satisfied with the outcome of the 1980 elections. As dean of the New Right in the Senate, he was in a position to see that his ideas were now taken seriously. He had demonstrated that he was not just a visionary with no capacity to wield power. The Congressional Club, an independent political action organization run by Helms's backers, had stood first among right-wing political action fund-raising groups with an expenditure of $4,601,069 for the Reagan campaign. (See note page 96.)

The National Conservative Political Action Committee, known as Nick-Pack, was the runner-up, expending $3,307,962, of which $1,859,168 was used in support of Mr. Reagan's candidacy. NCPAC had distinguished itself as the largest negative campaigner, using $1,435,232, not to support particular candidates or parties, but to discredit office-holders targeted for defeat. These negative campaigns by NCPAC and other independent political action groups, which often involved attacking the morality and patriotism of their victims, were most effective in defeating Senators Richard

Clark and Thomas MacIntyre in 1978, principally on the abortion issue, and successfully repeating the same tactics in 1980 against Senators Church, McGovern, Culver, Bayh, and others. Altogether, independent political action committees and individuals spent more than $16,000,000 in 1980, according to Federal Election Commission reports, most of which was for the benefit of conservative and right-wing candidates and issues. Based on these statistics, *New York Times* writer Adam Clymer found that Mr. Reagan's campaign had gained from the expenditure of $10,601,864, compared with $27,773 spent by independent P.A.C.s for Mr. Carter, a ratio of 382 to 1. The total raised and spent in 1980 by these committees and groups had increased eight times from the amount reported in the campaign of 1976. These monies, it must be understood, are in addition to the expenditures legally permitted by the political parties and official campaign organizations representing candidates.

American politics is therefore awash with money raised and spent outside the legally constituted campaigns.

Independent groups are immune from the law since they are deemed not to be under the direct control or influence of parties or candidates. They are responsible to no one except themselves, and the fact that they are not presumed to be part of a campaign tends to make their propaganda misleading and vicious. As we noted earlier, Senators Church and McGovern found their states flooded with antiabortion literature, attacking them in morally outrageous terms; the literature could not be traced back to any candidate or party organization.

When NCPAC opened its 1982 crusade against Senator Moynihan by broadcasting commercials attacking the Senator, the *New York Times* in its lead editorial of November 18, 1981, recalled the celebrated boast of NCPAC's organizer Terry Dolan: "A group like ours could lie through its teeth and the candidate it helps stays clean." The *Times* asked editorially:

Why shouldn't an independent group spend freely for candidates it likes? Because it's far from clear that Nick-Pack is either
independent or a group.

The organization doesn't consist of much besides Mr. Dolan,
a talented fund-raiser, and a board. As for independence . . .
[the candidate who benefits] may depend more on Nick-Pack
than vice versa, but the effect is the same either way: the
contribution limit is evaded.

The *Times* editorial understates the effect of this relationship. Not only is the legal limit on campaign contributions
skirted with impunity, but the unofficial nature of the
arrangement allows an independent P.A.C. to do the dirty
work of attacking a politician's image or reputation while his
opponent cannot be held responsible and may in many cases
truthfully claim total innocence. After all, how can one be
held responsible for what unauthorized groups say or do?
In Mr. Dolan's famous phrase, "the candidate . . . stays
clean." The exploitation of this gap in the law creates havoc
with political ethics and is casting a lengthening shadow on
the integrity of the American political process.

The problem of controlling this abuse poses a serious
constitutional difficulty for legislatures and the courts. Without infringing upon the right of free speech and a free press,
how can the law forbid citizens who are not running for office,
and not affiliated with those doing so, from mounting a
soapbox or hiring a printing press and saying whatever they
wish to say? On the other hand, how can democracy survive if
one contestant enters the ring alone, wearing the boxing
gloves prescribed by law, while his opponent climbs over the
ropes accompanied by a gang of political street fighters armed
with lead pipes and bicycle chains?

These are the odds when candidates and their parties fight
within the rules provided by law, while their opponents assail
them with a private army of financial backers and richly
funded campaigners. These were the handicaps suffered by
many candidates who faced the New Right in 1978 and 1980,

and right-wing stategists did not wait for the political funerals of their "targets" before announcing that they were already laying plans for more of the same in the campaigns of 1982 and '84, illustrated by NCPAC's opening effort against New York's Senator Moynihan.

Representative John H. Buchanan, Jr., of Alabama's sixth district, must have felt he was fighting bicycle chains and lead pipes when the Moral Majority weighed into the Republican primary in September 1980. Although a conservative Republican and an ordained Southern Baptist minister, Buchanan was chosen to receive Jerry Falwell's "treatment" because the congressman had outraged the New Right by favoring the Panama Canal treaty and supporting the extension for ratification of the Equal Rights Amendment. He was also thought to be too soft on military issues and social policy. In a media campaign Buchanan was accused of not being in favor of school prayer, although his record showed that he had once voted in favor of such a proposal. Falwell came to Alabama, attacking Buchanan at a Birmingham rally and appearing with his opponent on television. Meanwhile, Stuart Gaines, executive director of the Moral Majority of Alabama, assured the press that because of its nonprofit status, Moral Majority does not endorse candidates.

Despite his conservative legislative record and sixteen years experience in Congress, Representative Buchanan was defeated 55 percent to 45 percent. In a victory widely hailed as evidence of the religious New Right's coming of age, Gaines boasted, "We are going to broaden our base, be spectacularly large. . . . We intend to have an effect on government."

Buchanan's campaign manager, George Seaborne, claiming that the Moral Majority had persistently distorted the congressman's record, summarized his candidate's impossible position by saying: "There is no way to attack churches." The successful effort to unseat a conservative Republican congressman who did not bow to the militant right on foreign and military affairs or social issues had been organized largely through fundamentalist congregations, especially among Baptists, Presbyterians, and Churches of Christ and Churches of God. Campaign manager Seaborne observed: "In a fundamentalist church, what the preacher says is gospel. If the preacher says John Buchanan has an immoral record, not many are going to get hold of a copy of the *Congressional Record* to see what the vote was." The chairman of the Alabama Democratic Party summed up the alliance between the extreme right and fundamentalist religion with a remark to a *New York Times* reporter. The Moral Majority, he said, is "the John Birch Society wrapped in the flag of the church."

The unseating of an established conservative congressman was probably more important to the extreme right in asserting its influence than half a dozen victories over better-known liberals and moderates. After all, as Viguerie has made emphatic in his distinction between the "old" conservatives and the New Right, the old conservatives tend to be gentlemen and ladies who too often have lost elections. In contrast, the New Right, self-designated "radicals" in Weyrich's terms, are determined to forge the political weapons, weld the alliances, and raise the overwhelming sums of money required to gain and hold power.

The $16 million spent in 1980 by predominately rightist political action committees and individuals gives only a small part of the picture of right-wing resources. Many millions more are raised and allocated annually to support a constellation of tax-exempt foundations, so-called educational funds and think tanks controlled by the New Right and their allies. Their output ranges from scholarly studies by the American Enterprise Institute and similar conservative intellectual centers—much of their work of high quality and scholarly value—to blatant propaganda from right-wing mills that function as political action groups in all but name. Such operations maintain their tax-exempt status as not-for-profit educational foundations by stopping just short of what the law forbids.

No one has contributed to the building of the financial infrastructure of the New Right more than Richard Viguerie, who has turned direct mail political fund-raising into a profitable business, as well as the critical nexus of the new politics. The Viguerie group of companies in Falls Church, Virginia, employing 250 people, were by 1980 raising $35 to $40 million annually, according to observers. Using computerized mailing lists containing four-and-a-half million names, they have built a grass-roots network of right-wing activists and supporters. Viguerie refuses to confirm the total of his fund-raising effort, but according to E. J. Dionne, Jr. of the *New York Times*, he acknowledged that his gross profit was 12 percent.

Another unseen component of the New Right's financial armory consists of a cluster of privately endowed foundations, providing resources for conservative and rightist causes. Dan Morgan of the *Washington Post* investigated the extent to which private foundations are buttressing right-wing causes and quoted Leopold Tyrmand, himself part of the neoconservative network, as describing it as a "second culture" with "its own system of communications by way of newsletters, periodicals, scholarly journals, lecture circuits, academic organizations, literary reviews, conferences, seminars, etc." Morgan found that in some cases long established foundations that had originally used their funds for philanthropic purposes are switching support to rightist and conservative politics. He noted, for example, that ten years ago the Sarah Mellon Scaife Foundation, with assets of nearly $100 million, "gave mainly to traditional community causes such as the opera and the United Negro College Fund. Today its list of 'public affairs' recipients reads like a Who's Who of the conservative network, a shift reflecting the interests of Richard Mellon

Scaife, the foundation's chairman and a Republican campaign contributor."

A survey by the *Washington Post* found other corporate and individual benefactors of the network to include the John M. Olin Foundation, the Lilly Foundation, the J. Howard Pew Freedom Trust (Sun Oil), the Samuel Noble Foundation, and the Joseph Coors Foundation, which distributes its public affairs grants among programs in foreign affairs, conservative economics, media, and antienvironmental legal action. Corporate contributors identified by the *Post* included "Weyerhaeuser, Ford, Reader's Digest, Potlatch, Mobil, Coca Cola, Consolidated Foods, Ashland Oil, Tennessee Gas Transmission, Firestone, Pizza Hut, Castle and Cook, Hershey, Exxon, Citibank, Republic Steel, General Motors, Morgan Guaranty Trust, IBM, and many others."

What emerges is a political system vulnerable to distortion by money operating largely outside responsible party organizations or declared candidates, allied with extremist religious and ideological networks working almost invisibly through fundamentalist churches, and right-wing coalitions and publications. Conservatives no less than liberals are subject to their attacks and slanders, which seem to appear from nowhere and spread allegations they know to be misleading or false. Even when their misrepresentations are pointed out, these extremists commonly ignore the correction and repeat their offenses.

When the American nation turns to the ideological right, who are the people left behind? And who stand to gain? Certainly truth and respect for fair play are left behind. But it is perhaps easier to identify those who will lose than to know who the winners will be.

I have argued in previous chapters that the New Right ideology that strongly influences White House policy is not a basically conservative philosophy. It is not conservative in its approach to Constitutional rights, to social issues, to military policy, or to international relations. It is a hybrid, attempting to combine traditional American values with authoritarian and adventurist policies that are deeply offensive to personal freedom and a stable society. If this analysis is correct, authentic American conservatives should be as disturbed as social liberals and moderates at what is taking place. The surrealistic economic landscape only further confirms that neoconservatism as interpreted by the current New Right brain trust is seriously off track. Presidential candidate George Bush, then still free to speak his mind, was nearer the truth than he knew in characterizing as "voodoo economics" the prescription now being administered to the national economy. The American economy is several times larger than its nearest competitor, and what we do critically affects the world's economic health, as our Western allies keep reminding us. In the opinion of many economists, the shortsighted Smoot-Hawley tariff half a century ago tripped world trade dominoes and produced global depression; ill-conceived economic nostrums can once again devastate not only our own domestic prosperity, but prostrate the world as well.

Who stands to gain? The easy, assured answer generally given is inadequate. Business, the rich, or investment bankers are not certain winners. To think they are reflects partisan feeling more than economic reality. The only sure gainers are the New Right metaphysicians and hucksters who have attained power and glory in the wake of political triumph. But winning is not the same as governing. Even the President does not stand to gain if his merry pipers lead him and his Administration over the promontory and into the cold sea of an economic Arctic.

The slowness to respond to business and investment anxieties marks a mentality that is more ideological than pro-business. Business executives, when they are acting as professionals, put pragmatic judgment before ideological neatness. They may prefer lowering taxes and restricting government services, but if the result is an economy in which business cannot prosper, flexibility triumphs over theory and business agrees to tax increases or social programs as these measures are indicated. Ideologues, on the other hand, will wreck a national or a global economy rather than compromise the articles of their faith. The Reagan administration will be the stage for a continuing tug of war between ideologues and pragmatists.

On the eve of becoming the second black mayor of Atlanta, Andrew Young questioned the view that Federal policy was serving America's economic interest, or even the interests of the business groups who are reputed to be the beneficiaries of the prevailing policy. In an interview with *New York Times* reporters, Young commented that the Reagan Administration had succumbed to ideology to the point of failing to pursue policies that would benefit the business community and the nation's economy:

> Pragmatic businessmen would have realized the market potential around the world and would have begun to internationalize our economy to make it more competitive. But they are not business-oriented. . . . Supply-side economics is not a pragmatic business, something that has grown out of business practice.

At the heart of the problem Andrew Young describes is the difference between what is in the interest of a people or a group, and what they *perceive* as their interest. The distinction is unnoticed by those governed by ideology, whether of the left or the right. It is not in the interest of Americans to bring economic havoc to their land, to pit group against group and young against old for the glorification of a dubious theory: the proposition that by lowering taxes we necessarily increase economic vitality and promote social well-being. If it were invariably so, there would have been few panics or depressions during the first 150 years of American history. The Great Depression that brought Franklin Roosevelt to the

White House would have been impossible—unless we are to suppose that Harding, Coolidge, and Hoover were closet socialists undercutting free enterprise.

Ideologues are addicted to simple, uniform solutions. Each ideological creed has its own indubitable truths for which it is willing to sacrifice other people's welfare, and if necessary, their very lives. Thus the attempted raid on Social Security benefits, which people of small and modest means had confidently regarded as guaranteed by the faith and credit of the United States government, was thwarted only by an unexpectedly strong uprising by the victims whose pockets were to have been looted. The proposed drastic reduction of benefits for those retiring at sixty-two—which ignored the fact that many heavy industries required labors beyond the capacities of many workers past their early sixties—was not based on any defensible economic necessity or justification. Its motivation was ideological rather than financial or actuarial, designed to force people entitled to benefits to surrender their just claims on the altar of political theory. Even by conservative economic principles, it is bad policy to deprive people of the incentive to work, and Social Security is an earned credit for having worked. The radical right would destroy Social Security to spite the philosophy of governmental involvement in advancing social well-being.

The attack on the changing role of women, the rights of minorities, on liberals, humanists, educators, and scientists is at base an assault on any institution or association that enables people to resist dictation by this network—social authoritarians and militant nationalists, supported by defenders of narrowly held wealth, not even broadly representative of American capitalism, striving to secure permanent political dominance by reducing all likely challengers to impotence. The attack on labor unions, which proceeds apace through adoption state-by-state of "right-to-work" laws would, if successful, make labor malleable in the hands of managers and entrepreneurs. The prospect of success for such a retrogressive policy is greater than many people suppose, since the service industries of the future are much more difficult to unionize than the mining and heavy manufacturing industries that gave organized labor its first real chance in our history. Professional elites, functioning in a manner suggestive of the closed guilds of the Middle Ages, may come to compete with trade unionism as we have known it, leaving many trades and unskilled laborers unrepresented.

The National Right to Work Committee, headed by Reed Larson, admired by Viguerie as "an organizational genius who understands how to use, effectively, direct mail, newspaper ads, and other mass media," had grown spectacularly to more than a million and a half supporters by 1980, leading Viguerie to predict passage of right-to-work laws in several new states in the next few years. Viguerie, like other New Right architects, sees the union shop as a "form of slavery," which he would like to lift from the backs of labor. Already the union shop has been outlawed in some twenty of the nation's states. Together with the end of the union shop, the radical right is lobbying to outlaw unions for government workers, including teachers. Not only would unlawful strikes by key civil servants, such as air controllers, be forbidden, but union representation of government workers would be prohibited. The Family Protection Act proposes to put one aspect of this goal into effect by denying Federal aid to schools with unionized faculties.

The question who loses, or is left behind, when America turns to the doctrinaire right must be resolved by answering almost everybody—including traditional conservatives and all believers in a pluralistic free society. The democratic ideal is to enable all people, young and old, black and white, native and foreign-born, rich and poor, male and female, to gain the economic and political empowerment to represent themselves and direct their own lives. The doctrinaire right would betray this dream by restricting the nation's future to a narrowly conceived social and political order, called conservative, but actually involving forced uniformity and subordination of the individual to an elitist, militarized state and society. Such a social order, if it could last, would be managed by a circle of ideological puritans as mean-spirited and intellectually narrow as any group of zealots in our history. It is a fate Americans who love liberty must recognize as alien to our heritage and reject emphatically.

Author's Note: Statistics on expenditures of independent political action committees cited earlier in the chapter (from an article by Adam Clymer in the *New York Times*, November 29, 1981) refer to sums "not subject to any contribution or spending limit," as released the day before the *Times* article by the Federal Election Commission.

Statistics made public by the Commission on February 20, 1982, (as reported by Warren Weaver, Jr., *New York Times*, February 21, 1982) indicate a total of more than $131 million spent by political action committees on the 1980 campaign—up from $77.4 million for the election two years earlier. These statistics, many times larger than those reported in the Clymer article, include contributions to Senate and House candidates, the latter being the chief beneficiaries. The February 1982 report listed the National Conservation Political Action Committee as the largest spender, at $7.5 million, with the National Congressional Club second, at $7.2 million.

The Weaver article also noted that the 1980 presidential and congressional elections cost the Republican Party $170 million, compared with the $35 million spent by the Democrats, a ratio of nearly five to one.

9

AMERICA'S DEMOCRATIC HERITAGE:

Secular and Free

America's constitutional foundation as a secular, pluralistic democracy, in which every philosophy and faith can exist with maximum freedom and equality, is no historical accident. It is the outcome of a profound moral and philosophical revolution that required generations to come to fruition. While today's liberalism is different in style and application from that of Locke or Jefferson, its essential principles and approach to government and society remain unchanged after the vicissitudes of three hundred years.

Despite neoconservative claims that today's liberalism has come to a deadend, or that in a slide toward totalitarianism, it has abandoned its historical ground as the essential philosophy of freedom, liberal philosophy is still vital and uniquely expressive of constitutional free government. While its mutable fashions and preoccupations are highly transient, as seen in the causes and styles of the 1960s and early 70s, the underlying structures and spirit of liberal philosophy are as enduring as free government itself. When the liberal spirit dies, democracy will die with it.

The Reverend James Robison enthusiastically attacks humanism and liberalism in American life as the sources of moral rebellion and social degeneracy. In a sentence that even in the company of the radical right is outstanding for lack of perspicacity, Mr. Robison declared himself "sick and tired hearing about all the radicals and the perverts and the liberals and the leftists and the Communists coming out of the closet."

The bracketing of "liberals," whose philosophical and religious ranks must include such figures as Locke, Hume, Jefferson, Franklin, Madison and Lincoln—and in basics Washington as well—with those whom Mr. Robison classifies as morally perverse and anti-American so defies reason as to be impervious to argument.

But if we must choose between Robison's notion of the foundations of the American Constitution and the assumptions of the founders, the choice should not be difficult to make. The threat to intellectual and religious freedom in America today springs from widespread ignorance of our history of ideas, specifically of the philosophy that provides the foundation for the pluralistic secular democracy imbedded in our Constitution.

As we have insisted throughout this book, liberalism is not to be understood as a merely partisan creed, even though many today use the word exclusively in this sense. There are many political and economic factions and programs that historically have been labeled as liberal, with their content changing from period to period and place to place. We have also rejected classifying liberalism as the opposite of conservatism. As observed previously, some forms of conservatism are indeed authoritarian or even totalitarian, and therefore antiliberal in the root sense. But in societies such as the United States, and generally throughout the English-speaking world, the prevailing conservative heritage is anti-authoritarian, that is to say, based on historic liberal social principles.

There is nothing frivolous in observing that most conservatives in the United States and other democracies are within the great tradition of philosophical liberalism. Winston Churchill, for example, led the Conservative Party in Britain, but on the fundamental constitutional issues of British law Churchill stood with the liberal tradition of John Locke and the Glorious Revolution of 1688, which put away the autocratic power of kings ruling by divine right and advanced the idea of government based on the consent of the governed, government by social contract.

While Churchill's party had assimilated these changes sometimes grudgingly, the fact remains that British Conservatives were as deeply offended by the rise of modern totalitarianism in the form of fascism as any English or American liberal or radical democrat. In similar fashion, progressive liberals and humanists such as Bertrand Russell and John Dewey, together with such political figures as Franklin D. Roosevelt—and even democratic socialists of the character of Harold Laski and Norman Thomas—recoiled from the totalitarian party of Lenin and Stalin, rejecting the pretension by a revolutionary elite of the historic right to capture power and govern by autocratic means.

What is modern totalitarianism but the divine right of kings resurrected in a more virulent strain to proclaim the right of a self-chosen minority to install itself as the vanguard of history? Liberalism stands historically against all such pretensions to power, whether they are mounted from left or right.

Unlike the authentic constitutional conservative, the authoritarian right-winger is contemptuous of this philosophical heritage and repudiates or gravely impairs the constitutional restraints that the liberal revolution placed on government's power to shackle conscience and reason. In his departure from this tradition the neoauthoritarian betrays fascistic rather than genuine conservative traits.

Although the roots of liberal philosophy extend to ancient times and can be seen in many of the heresies of the Middle Ages, it is from the Renaissance and the period during and following the Reformation that we see clearly its modern development.

The philosophy of John Locke often serves as the zero milestone on the grand highway of a fully developed philosophy of liberalism, taking Locke's great *Essay Concerning Human Understanding*, published in 1689, as the epochal event in our intellectual history. This followed by one year the removal of the last of the Stuart kings in the Whig revolution of 1688. By putting an end to absolutist pretentions in Britain, the Whigs set in motion the forces that shaped the American Revolutionary philosophy in its complementary liberal and conservative aspects.

The British Whig, therefore, is the common ancestor, the founder of a tradition that makes today's authentic conservative and genuine liberal members of the same philosophical family. This history goes far to explain why Americans of differing economic and social philosophies have been able to maintain a democratic system with frequent peaceful changes of administration, throughout the conflicts and tensions of two hundred years. Only the crisis of the slave question ruptured the give and take of constitutional government.

The path from John Locke and the Whig Revolution of 1688 to Thomas Jefferson and the Declaration of 1776 is an undulating but unbroken line. Behind the social and political history of the American Revolution stood the moral and intellectual revolution from which Jefferson, Madison, and the other major architects of American freedom drew their inspiration.

What force did these philosophers of the seventeenth and eighteenth centuries unleash that so mightily transformed history? Essentially they did an about-face from the doctrine of human nature that had prevailed for most of Christian history. They denied that human nature is essentially evil; they affirmed the human capacity for self-government, and they provided the moral foundation for a reasonable belief in human freedom and progress.

How, they asked, do we distinguish good from evil? What is the basis of morality and ethics? The orthodox religious answer had always been divine revelation. We can know the good only as God has revealed it to us through his prophets. Moses had received his tablets of the Law on Sinai. In Christian ethical thought God had delivered his moral law through a succession of seers culminating in the advent of Christ. Scripture, interpreted by an authoritative church, was the final depository of moral truth. Theocracy follows as the logical government derived from such a moral philosophy.

Although most of the liberal thinkers of the late seventeenth and eighteenth centuries believed in a Supreme Being as the first cause, and were either deists or liberal Christians, they turned their backs on the ancient authorities of scripture and priesthood as the necessary depositories of moral knowledge. They reasoned that ancient holy books were fallible and could be further corrupted in transmission, while priesthoods were often self-serving and oppressive.

In effect, they concluded, we have no need for such uncertain and arbitrary authorities, which would keep the mind enslaved. The only revelation of the moral law we require, they argued, comes from an understanding of nature and human reason. By studying nature, including the social nature of humankind, we can discover the principles of morality and thus equip ourselves to live as morally free beings.

This was a bold declaration of spiritual independence, and on this foundation the liberal philosophy and secular constitutional democracy were constructed in their modern form.

Jefferson welcomed this moral philosophy because it set the mind free. He believed that as our knowledge of psychology and of social behavior increases, we are better able to understand nature, including moral nature.

One of the most influential of this line of philosophers, the Earl of Shaftesbury, whose early education had been guided by Locke, insisted that the moral sense is part of our makeup as social beings, inherent in our natures. Sympathy for others is its natural foundation. From social feelings for other life we develop and refine our morality.

A freethinker in matters of religion, Shaftesbury considered religious doctrine to be harmful to moral development if it teaches us to despise human nature or proposes to ground morality on a theology of future rewards and punishment. If people behave in an approved way in order to avoid punishment either here on earth or in hell afterward, said Shaftesbury, they are not behaving as moral beings. They are acting as slaves or subjects driven by fear, and in so behaving they are denied the chance to become fully human as morally conscious beings.

It is when we know and do the right out of a love for the morally worthy act, the generous compassionate act, that we become in the proper sense moral beings. No priesthood or ancient source of miracle reveals this knowledge to us. We find the genesis of moral behavior in our inherent capacity to feel the pains and fears of others and to extend sympathy and caring to our fellow beings. This philosophy of ethics has been called the "moral sense" school, after Shaftesbury's introduction of the term.

Toward the middle of the eighteenth century, David Hartley followed Shaftesbury in rejecting the notion that morality can properly be based on an expectation of divine rewards and punishments. Hartley objected so strongly to the doctrine of eternal sanctions that he abandoned his studies for the Anglican priesthood at Cambridge and became a physician instead. Although he remained a liberal member of the Church of England and shared with the deists a belief in God as the first cause, he saw no need to base his moral philosophy on scripture or ecclesiastical authority.

He agreed with Shaftesbury that morality is properly understood as resting on the human capacity of sympathy for others, for what today we would call altruism; but Hartley disagreed with Shaftesbury's belief that the moral sense is inherent or instinctive. Instead, Hartley argued, we learn it. What we know as the moral sense is the outcome of our social experience as infants and children.

To show how this develops he returned to a conception of the mind that John Locke had offered. Before we experience sensations, said Locke, the human mind is a blank tablet. Through the experience of the senses and the association of impressions into ideas the mind takes form. This, said Hartley, is also how moral conceptions develop. Beginning in early infancy with immediate concern for our selfish needs, we grow, if we are loved, into an awareness of others and a feeling of sharing in their welfare. Out of our sympathetic relationships we develop a moral consciousness, a feeling of reciprocal obligation. Thus, as Jefferson later observed, an atheist can be, and often is, as morally good as any believer. Being a person formed in a relationship of mutual caring and trust is more decisive in shaping character than moral indoctrination or theology.

Shaftesbury's view that morality is based on the social nature of human beings, and is thus open to discovery and rational examination, was adopted by moral philosophers within the church as well as by non-Christian deists. One of the former, Francis Hutcheson, who early in his career had received a license to preach, was accused before the Glasgow presbytery in 1738 of "following two false and dangerous doctrines: first, that the standard of moral goodness was the promotion of the happiness of others; and second, that we could have the knowledge of good and evil without a prior knowledge of God."

Hutcheson was not dissuaded. From his chair of moral philosophy at the University of Glasgow, he continued to develop the line of thought suggested by Shaftesbury. His ethical theories in turn found varied expression in the systems of Hume, Reid, Adam Smith, and other eighteenth-century Scottish thinkers whose ideas played an exceptional part in Jefferson's philosophical development.

These moral philosophers were endeavoring to discover some general principle that would unify moral experience in the same way that Isaac Newton's laws of gravity unified physical nature. Both efforts were denounced by the orthodox and fundamentalists of their day as godless, Newton for daring to explain the motion of the heavens by physical principles and John Locke and his successors for attempting to uncover a psychological ground in human nature to account for the origin of the moral feelings.

Hartley's view of moral development was adopted by Joseph Priestley, the amateur scientist who discovered oxygen, who by vocation was a dissenting clergyman of liberal (Unitarian) theological and social views. Priestley transmitted Hartley's moral philosophy to his close friend and admirer, Thomas Jefferson. The philosophical friendship that grew between Priestley and Jefferson is superbly described by the American historian Daniel J. Boorstin in *The Lost World of Thomas Jefferson*, the story of the gifted circle that made up Jefferson's intellectual community.

While Jefferson stands out boldly as the most philosophically literate of the architects of American freedom (with at least Madison receiving far less public recognition than he deserves), Jefferson was not alone in his attachment to religious liberalism and tolerance. Franklin, Madison, Monroe, the Adamses, and Washington were all heterodox or "liberal" in their religious beliefs and firmly committed to the creation of a secular government that might be independent of ecclesiastical ties or theological sanctions.

Among the founders, ironically, it is the first among them who is generally underrated in history as a shaper of ideas. The cold, austere image of Washington the soldier and the aristocratic President stiffening to command foreign and domestic respect for the fledgling office has eclipsed a passionate and lively mind of considerable power. The familiar image of General Washington kneeling in prayer in the snow at Valley Forge hides the freethinker and rationalist. Washington shared with the cultivated deists of his century a belief in a Creator who had designed and set in motion the machinery of the universe. But such a deity did not intervene miraculously in history and revealed himself only through the perfect regularities of nature. Thus, holy books, prophets, and messiahs were the products of human invention and in fact represented a denial of the sufficiency of the Creator's original design.

James Thomas Flexner, whose four-volume biography of Washington stands as one of the most detailed and careful studies of his life and thought, states unequivocally that Washington was not a believer in the Christian religion. He never took communion and when pressured to do so, decided to absent himself from church services. As a wealthy planter he served on the vestry of the local Anglican parish, a civic responsibility expected of one of his social standing, but confined his functions to the secular affairs of the legally established church body.

Like other cultivated freethinkers of his time and station, Washington believed in the utility of organized religion in serving the spiritual needs of the common folk and in maintaining respect for law and public order; but Washington's own inspiration and moral guidance came from another source. He followed the tradition of the Roman Stoics, especially Marcus Aurelius, who provided a model of self-control and service to nation and humanity.

The stoics saw human conscience as reflective of a divine spark in the nature of things, and this concept gave Washington the maxim by which he guided his conduct and recommended the moral life to others: "Labor to keep alive in your breast that little spark of celestial fire—conscience."

While Washington's strenuous exertions for self-improvement and mastery of the stoic virtues may in our more relaxed and egalitarian age contribute to his image of dreary rectitude, he is hardly less appealing than Jefferson in the breadth of his religious sympathy and respect for differences. Like Jefferson he sided with the suffering Baptist folk of Virginia as they endured punishment for resisting conformity to the established church; he noted the advantage of toleration practiced by Pennsylvania; he wrote warm hospitable letters to Jewish congregations with whom he registered an obvious religious affinity; he was tolerant of Catholics, and of John Murray's infant Universalist Church (now part of the Unitarian Universalist Association), which scandalized the orthodox with its denial of everlasting hell and its distinctive tenet that all human souls would finally be reconciled to God in universal salvation.

When Quaker conscientious objectors in Virginia were marched two hundred miles with guns strapped on their backs, a horrified Washington released the captives, sending them home with an expression of respect for those who were "scrupulously conscientious" in resisting war. (This was the same Washington who, first tasting battle in the opening skirmishes of the French and Indian War had reported, "I heard the bullets whistle, and . . . there is something charming in the sound," a cockiness that is said by Walpole to have brought George II to remark: "He would not say so, if he had been used to hear many.")

Washington supported religious freedom for all. Despite

the fact that he is not remembered as an intellectual, in his recent biographer's judgment he showed respect for intellectual values, for disinterested public service, and for a pragmatic approach to the problems of government.

When the partisans of the radical right denounce liberal moral philosophy as godless and perverse, we should remember that their ideological ancestors were shouting the same abuse at the likes of Jefferson and Madison and before them Hartley, Hume, Hutcheson, Shaftesbury, and Locke, two and three hundred years ago. Joseph Priestley's laboratory and library in Birmingham, England, were burned by a mob representing the "moral" majority of that generation, forcing the celebrated scientist and theologian to flee to America for his safety.

Progress and freedom are always godless to the lovers of darkness and superstition. Jefferson answered them for all time: "Reason and free inquiry are the only effectual agents against error. Give a loose to them, they will support the true religion by bringing every false one to their tribunal, to the test of their investigation. They are the natural enemies of error only."

The authoritarian mind, in both its religious and secular guises, fears and hates the searchlight of human reason and inquiry and throughout history has sought to extinguish that light, and for good reason: because authoritarianism knows its shabby claim to represent the voice of God cannot be sustained, except where truth is blinded and reason silenced.

During his campaigns for president, Jefferson was denounced as an atheist and a Jacobin—the equivalent of calling him a Communist today. Jefferson replied in a letter to a friend, with reference to the clergy who were mounting this attack upon his person and philosophy: "They believe that any portion of power confided in me will be exerted in opposition to their schemes. And they believe rightly; for I have sworn upon the altar of God eternal hostility against every form of tyranny over the mind of man."

Despite the effort to represent liberalism as a philosophy without a clear moral foundation, its philosophical history proves otherwise. It shares with the great religions and ethical philosophies of humanity commitment to the worth and sanctity of the person as a moral being. Many religious and philosophical sources have contributed to this conception of human life.

The virtue of the liberal humanistic tradition lies in this very recognition of universal human experience. The liberal moral philosophy does not see itself as a closed ideology or insular morality standing in opposition to other traditions. Ethical universalism is the very essence of the liberal spirit. To be consistent in this belief, compassion and caring must extend to all of our fellow beings; the moral feelings cannot be reserved for members of any one church, party, nation or race.

Many have tried to make religion, race, nationality, or politics the basis upon which they segregate their fellow beings from themselves, denying the moral equality and dignity of those on the far side of the divide. But this effort will always fail, and at great cost in human life and suffering. Whether we learn this lesson soon enough will most certainly determine whether the human race can survive in a nuclear age.

As Shaftesbury and his philosophical successors recognized, caring and compassion are the very roots that nurture our moral experience and make us human. We need not look elsewhere to find the source of morality. Whether we are discussing the intimate relationship between a man and a woman, or the ties between and among nations, the basis of the moral life remains human sympathy. Whatever demeans, degrades, or denies the dignity of any member of the human community threatens the relationship and undermines the moral life. Between individuals the consequences of this breakdown can be serious indeed. Lives are diminished or wasted, and occasionally callous and exploitative relationships result in the violence and sensational murders reported in the media. Among nations at each other's throats, or in holy wars between antagonistic religions or ideologies, the struggle can destroy civilization and exterminate humanity itself.

The extreme religious right has made much of rapidly changing sexual codes; when fundamentalist leaders charge that social liberalism and humanism deny morality, they are blaming humanism for evolving social patterns that, in their static view of things, can only be seen as evil. But a change of sexual patterns and standards of conduct does not mean moral collapse, or indicate that emerging patterns of morality are necessarily inferior. Certainly it should be clear that many traditional mores have become arbitrary and inappropriate.

A more humanistic morality means a more reasoned and thoughtful morality, a sense of responsibility that keeps in view the human purpose to be served. Obviously such a morality demands more of human beings than a doctrine that simply lays down a list of rigid rules and taboos, saying this you must do, and that you must not do.

A philosophy of humanism demands more. It requires us to take responsibility for our lives in the full knowledge that our long-term happiness and the needs and rights of those closest to us depend upon our decency and caring. Thus, while customs and mores change—and must change—the obligation to maximize the dignity of life and quality of human relationships remains a moral constant.

As a moral philosophy resting on liberal premises, humanism is an untenable position for anyone who holds an essentially negative view of human freedom. The ethics of humanism requires the same gamble on the ability of human beings to govern themselves that democracy requires in the sphere of politics. It is no accident that those in our history who advocated reason and free inquiry with respect to government, as we have seen from Locke to Jefferson, argued also for the use of freedom and reason in moral philosophy and religion.

Liberal moral philosophy is essentially the antiauthoritarian mind applied to questions of conduct. For this reason the new authoritarians have focused their attacks on humanistic education and religious liberalism. Authoritarians have never been comfortable with the proposition that public morality can have its basis in everyday human experience and that it is therefore not only possible but necessary to base our civic morality and law upon public principles of rational inquiry and personal rights.

The new authoritarians tell us that if we do not accept their conception of morality, a conception based on the presumption that they alone possess the key to decipher truth, we are to be regarded as "treacherous" individuals who must be driven from public life.

Many Americans will remember the years of McCarthyism, referred to at the beginning of this volume, when Joseph McCarthy and his followers attempted to use religious conformity as a test of patriotism. Adlai Stevenson, a Unitarian, confronted scurrilous attacks on his religion and personal morals when he became the Democratic candidate for president in 1952. Stevenson was further savaged for having as one of his advisors, Arthur Schlesinger, Jr., who was denounced as a "humanist." The Sunday newspaper supplements carried popular articles by J. Edgar Hoover, then chief of the F.B.I., deploring agnosticism and atheism, and attempting to link these views to Communism and subversion.

The leaders of Soviet Communism have been ruthless in advancing their totalitarian creed. History also records countless Christian and Muslim zealots and conquistadors who displayed equal cruelty and hatred of freedom. It is the spirit of absolutist fanaticism itself that a free people must resist. Our liberal democratic heritage, expressed in the American constitutional framework of secular, limited government, is our strongest bulwark for personal liberty and human rights.

AFTERWORD:
What Must We Do?

The historic alliance of liberal and evangelical forces, joined in support of freedom of thought and the separation of church and state, brought into being and sustains our pluralistic secular democracy. Ignorance of this tradition poses an increasing danger as deserters from their own spiritual heritage attempt to fashion a quasipolitical "moral majority." While these forces pay lip service to religious pluralism and the separation of church and state, the politics they promote would seriously violate the integrity and vitality of both. Faced with this challenge, evangelicals and liberals must become more keenly aware of their common interest in renewing commitment to the First Amendment.

Intellectual freedom in the teaching of science, the humanities, and social studies is imperative for a nation that is not to decline into a second- or third-rate power. America's influence as a force for freedom requires the moral and technological vitality that only a spirit of free inquiry can sustain. Protecting the integrity of science and improving the quality of science teaching in the United States, free from ideological or religious control, must be a common concern of all friends of public education.

Tolerance is not merely the absence of sectarian prejudices. In the long run a tolerant society is one in which diversity is prized as a necessary condition for freedom and social progress. Teachers must not be forced into a common mold, and while it is improper for teachers to indoctrinate students into a particular religious or ideological viewpoint, it is equally wrong to try to force educators into conformity to a politically imposed social or moral orthodoxy. Democracy in education requires development in students of critical skills, the ability to question, reason, and explore various options— capacities that teachers cannot elicit or encourage if they themselves lack these qualities or fear to express them. Americans who recognize the necessity for maintaining education of this quality must mobilize in its defense at national, state, and local levels.

Americans must understand more clearly than ever that democracy in our national experience has always meant pluralism, cultural diversity, freedom of choice in moral decisions that do not intrude upon the rights of others, and strict limitations on the power of the state to invade essentially private or personal matters of conscience or life-style. American democracy has never meant "tyranny of the majority" or what political scientists have aptly termed "totalitarian democracy." The founders of the nation wrote a Constitution designed to restrain the powers of government, even when acting in response to the popular will to tyrannize minorities or to exact conformity to mass opinion. It is therefore dismaying that many Americans fail to see the essential monstrosity of such concepts as a "moral majority" or "Christian America."

Liberal philosophy in all of its permutations over three centuries has been constant in recognizing pluralism and constitutionalism as both the means and the ends of a free democratic society. As we have insisted throughout this book, liberals and conservatives share equally in this heritage. Schoolchildren have not been educated to understand the foundations of freedom if they equate democracy with the simple proposition that popular might makes right; not even the might of a majority can make right the suppression of individuals or minorities who ought to be free in their persons and their private associations. True moral democracy in the historic constitutional sense is always a morality of diversity, liberty, and civic tolerance.

Finally, the secular democratic state is the surest protector of religious and intellectual liberty ever crafted by human ingenuity. Nothing is more fallacious, or more inimical to genuine religious liberty, than the seductive notion that the state should "favor" or "foster" religion. All history testifies that such practices inevitably result in favoring one religion over others, or fostering a combination of dominant religions over less powerful minorities and secular opinion. In the long run governmental favoritism vitiates the religious spirit itself. Where in the Western world is organized religion stronger than in the United States where the church is a take-your-choice affair? Where is it weaker than in Europe where sophisticated secularists joke that they have been "inoculated" for life against religion by compulsory religious indoctrination in state schools? Preserving the secular character of government and the public school is the surest guarantee that religion in America will remain free, vital, uncorrupted by political power, and independent of state manipulation.

To perpetuate and strengthen the foregoing values and principles, American citizens have organized themselves into many voluntary associations, from PTAs to better the public schools to councils of churches to foster interfaith understanding and community service. To assure that American freedom shall not die in our generation, Americans must continue to become involved in the voluntary civic activity that Tocqueville saw a century and a half ago as the source of our national genius.

In the course of this volume we have mentioned only a few of the many valuable organizations that defend American pluralism and personal freedom: The American Civil Liberties Union, the National Council of Churches of Christ in America, B'nai B'rith, the American Jewish Congress, the Baptist Joint Committee on Public Affairs, Catholics for a Free Choice, Planned Parenthood, the National Coalition for Democracy in Education, the American Ethical Union, the American Humanist Association, and the Unitarian Universalist Association, among others.

We could add such outstanding groups as the National Coalition Against Censorship, the American Library Association, Americans United for the Separation of Church and State, the National Education Association, the American Federation of Teachers, the National Organization of Women, the American Jewish Committee, People for the American Way, Americans for Common Sense, and various writers' groups. One group that deserves special mention is the Seventh Day Adventist Church, a Christian body that shares with Judaism Sabbatarian observance and that has waged a heroic struggle against Sunday blue laws and, more broadly, in support of voluntary religion free from state interference. Even the quixotic and often scorned Jehovah's Witnesses deserve the thanks of their fellow Americans for spirited defense of the right to be different; considering oaths of allegiance and "flag worship" to be idolatry, Witnesses have endured prison and flogging by "patriots" to win some of the most important constitutional cases in our century for freedom of conscience.

My good friend Roy Torcaso, the Maryland atheist and self-styled religious humanist (one of the most rigorously honest people I have ever known), who refused to affirm belief in a Supreme Being and a future state of rewards and punishments in order to qualify as an officer of the state (notary public), made freedom of conscience more secure for all Americans when a unanimous Supreme Court decided in his favor in *Torcaso vs. Watkins*. Many other champions of the struggle come to mind that limitations of space do not allow mentioning. If the Falwells, Robisons, Robinsons, and their bedfellows bothered to get acquainted with these diverse people and fathomed the depth and range of their sincerity and integrity—and if you and I did the same—we might all enrich our moral consciousness and appreciation of human courage.

As a final note, I might add two other initiatives to unite Americans of different religious and philosophical views into broadly based organizations in support of religious and intellectual freedom in America. The Center for Moral Democracy, a nonsectarian cooperative effort to stimulate a national grassroots movement "to preserve religious, intellectual and moral freedom within a constitutional secular democracy" was organized early in 1981, following a series of public platforms and a large rally convened by the New York Society for Ethical Culture with the co-sponsorship of a coalition of Protestant, Jewish, Unitarian Universalist, and humanist leaders. The Center has its national headquarters at 2 West 64th Street, New York City, 10023; the present writer initiated the Center and serves as its Director. Closely paralleling the Center in purpose and grassroots structure is a movement centered in Michigan and organized by Rabbi Sherwin Wine, founder of the Society for Humanistic Judaism. Known as the "Voice of Reason," Rabbi Wine's organization is also nonsectarian and committed to preservation of a constitutional secular state and public school. As these words are written, discussions are under way to merge the Voice of Reason and the Moral Democracy Center into a single nationwide effort.

The organizations mentioned above only illustrate the wide spectrum of opinion that remains loyal to the Jeffersonian ideal. Jefferson said it best for his generation and our own:

I consider the government of the United States as interdicted by the Constitution from intermeddling with religious institutions, their doctrines, disciplines or exercises. . . . I never will, by any word or act, bow to the shrine of intolerance, or admit a right of inquiry into the religious opinions of others. On the contrary, we are bound, you, I, and every one, to make common cause, even with error itself, to maintain the common right of freedom of conscience.